GLORIA HARGREAVES is one of Britain's leading graphologists and has assisted companies around the world in the selection of personnel. She regularly undertakes tours on the *QE2* and has made a number of television appearances. Her previous publications include *A Dictionary of Doodles*, *The Lovers' Handbook* and *How They Write*, featuring the handwriting of nearly 150 famous people.

PEGGY WILSON studied with Gloria Hargreaves and is now an experienced graphologist in her own right.

Also by Gloria Hargreaves

How They Write: Secrets of the
Famous Revealed

The Lovers' Handbook: Handwriting and
Personal Relationships

A Dictionary of Doodles

Gloria Hargreaves and Peggy Wilson

A DICTIONARY
OF GRAPHOLOGY

THE
A–Z
OF YOUR PERSONALITY

PETER OWEN · LONDON

PETER OWEN PUBLISHERS
73 Kenway Road London SW5 0RE

First published 1983
First published in this edition 1991
Copyright © Gloria Hargreaves and Peggy Wilson 1983, 1991

ISBN 0–7206–0631–4

A catalogue record for this book is available from
the British Library

Printed in Great Britain by Billings of Worcester

Contents

Introduction

What is graphology?

Graphology is the study of handwriting characteristics for the purpose of determining the personality of the writer. The fact that no two handwritings, not even those of identical twins, are the same has led graphologists over the years to investigate the precise relationship between character and handwriting. Little is known about the history of graphology before 1622, when the first printed work – by Camillo Baldi, a doctor of medicine and philosophy (and professor at the University of Bologna) – appeared in Italy, but it is thought that Chinese scholars already showed an interest in the subject over eight centuries ago. Modern graphology has its origins in France, the acknowledged founder being Jean Michon, who first used the word 'graphology' to describe his work. The results of his many years of research into handwriting characteristics were first published in 1872. From then on interest in the subject spread through Europe, with published works by notable graphologists such as Georg Meyer, Ludwig Klages, Max Pulver and Robert Saudek, who was particularly interested in the differences in national copybook styles and their relation to national character. In the present century the study of handwriting has been greatly helped by discoveries in psychology, and there is now an established body of knowledge on which handwriting analysis is based.

What does it reveal?

When we first learn to write we conform to a specific style, referred to by graphologists as 'copybook'. Gradually, as we develop, we begin to deviate in varying degrees from copybook and evolve a style that is uniquely our own. The extent of this variation is taken as the measure of the writer's individuality, maturity, originality, intelligence, ethical standards and general lifestyle. All these

7

aspects of the personality can be discovered by a careful study of the principal handwriting features – size, slant, speed, pen pressure, layout, forms of connection, broadness or narrowness, etc.

What are its limitations?

Certain kinds of information are not available to the graphologist by looking at a handwriting sample. One of these is the writer's age. A person's actual age is often at variance with his mental age. Examples of script produced at different stages of life will show the effect of experience on character and the development towards maturity. Writing, though a physical act, is largely a mental exercise and will therefore tend to show only the mental age of the writer. Similarly, it is difficult to determine the sex of the writer from a sample, partly because we all have masculine as well as feminine traits in our makeup. As both age and sex clearly have a bearing on the character analysis it is best to establish these at the start.

Another fact that is not apparent from the writing sample is left-handedness. It makes very little difference to the basic characteristics of the script which hand is used. A left-handed person will adjust his paper to produce a right slant if this comes naturally to him. People who have lost the use of one or both hands and have had to learn to write with the other hand, or with their feet, will develop a writing style that closely resembles their earlier one, unless their personality has changed as a result of the experience.

Nor, contrary to popular belief, can handwriting tell us anything about the future. It can only indicate the writer's potential and give an estimate of his future performance in different areas – social, domestic, professional – based on the qualities and abilities displayed in the writing. Graphologists are not endowed with some form of psychic power, although a measure of intuition can be extremely helpful.

In short, graphology does not claim to supply all the answers. Like psychoanalysis it should not be thought of as an exact science. It is based on certain acknowledged principles, which are open to variation in application and interpretation. Much depends on the individual graphologist, not only in arriving at an interpretation but in conveying his discoveries in language that is clearly understood by the person seeking the analysis.

Why a dictionary?

Graphology is now used not only by individuals trying to gain a better understanding of themselves but also increasingly in such fields as employment selection, vocational and marriage guidance, medicine, education, criminology and the law. Many books have been written on the subject, either about general principles of analysis or about one or more specialized areas, but these are often either too obscure or too limited in range. We felt that there was an urgent need for a book that made available much of the basic knowledge accumulated over the years in a way that was clear, easily accessible, and useful to a wide range of people – professional and lay, skilled and relatively inexperienced. Graphologists, graphology students, workers in other professions, as well as the layman whose interest in the subject is only just beginning, should all find useful information, new insights and even some light-hearted entertainment in these pages.

How to use the dictionary

The dictionary is divided into three parts: an A–Z of letter forms, a list of character traits and a glossary. These can be consulted individually for quick reference, or used in combination when making a more detailed analysis.

The *A–Z* sets out all the letters of the alphabet, both capital and small, and illustrates the great variety of ways in which they can be written. Each example is accompanied by a description of the letter formation and the character qualities this reveals. It is obviously not practicable to include every known variation, but we believe we have given enough examples to enable the reader to find an approximation to what he is looking for. It should be pointed out that before arriving at any conclusions readers should check whether letters are consistently formed in a certain way – indicating the presence of a definite personality trait – or whether they appear in two or three different forms, in which case the version repeated most often must be taken as representing the dominant trait. When attempting to form a picture of a person's character it is important not to rely on an analysis of individual letters alone but to look at a fuller writing sample and to check the evidence offered there against the list of character traits and the glossary.

The section on *character traits* lists a wide variety of individual qualities (from 'abrupt' to 'zestful') and matches each with an average of four to six handwriting characteristics. If three or four of these appear constantly in the handwriting sample it can be assumed that the matching character trait forms a definite part of the personality; if all are present it can be concluded that the trait is indeed a dominant one. A sample will often contain what might appear to be contradictory character traits. This is not surprising. It is extremely rare to find a person with a completely consistent character; most people have a mixture of positive and negative qualities.

The *glossary*, also arranged alphabetically, explains all the graphological terms referred to in the rest of the book. Illustrated examples are given in a separate column wherever appropriate. The experienced graphologist may wish to consult this section as a quick reminder of the significance of certain features. The beginner, on the other hand, will turn to it for essential information about the principles that form the basis of any serious investigation of handwriting and the role they play when making personality assessments. He will gain practical experience by applying this knowledge to actual handwriting samples and, with the aid of the other two sections, may attempt further steps in the direction of a proper handwriting analysis.

Some points of special interest

Additional information about a writer can be gained by comparing the signature with the rest of the script. If there is a considerable difference between the two the signature indicates the way the writer wishes to appear to others, whilst the script reveals the real person. Conversely, where signature and script match closely we can be assured that the writer is genuine, direct and unpretentious. Analysis of a signature alone will not necessarily give a true picture of the personality. The personal pronoun 'I' is also revealing; it shows what the writer feels about himself in relation to others. It should therefore be studied carefully, with particular reference to its size, slant and pressure.

Finally, it is worth pointing out to the would-be graphologist that at some point he will almost certainly meet someone who declares that he is in the habit of producing two, or even three, distinctly different writing styles. The answer is that, on closer examination, these differences will prove to be only superficial, the result of variations in mood, emotions, health or vitality, while the basic characteristics remain unchanged. Our handwriting may vary slightly from day to day or even from year to year, but rarely to the extent that our friends do not recognize it. It is the task of the graphologist to reveal the true personality hiding behind the smokescreen and it is the continuing fascination of this exercise that we believe will catch and hold the readers of this book.

A–Z

A

A	Low crossbar	Subordination
A	High crossbar	Superiority
A	Open at top	Sincerity, talkativeness
A	Narrow	Shyness, inhibition
A	Hooked starting stroke	Avarice, greed
A	Starting with spot at baseline	Enjoyment of material success; possible 'skeleton in cupboard'
A	Crossbar looped to left	Pride in achievements
A	Crossed at top	Non-conformity
	Sharp angles on starting and endstroke	Hardness, resentment

Λ	Crossbar omitted	Carelessness, absentmindedness
A	Starting stroke over-extended to left	Strong attachment to the past
a	Capital written as a small letter	Modesty
A	Descending crossbar	Disappointment
A	Enrolled on right	Egoism
Q	Circles within circles	Fixed ideas; lives in a world of his own
A	Additional stroke before crossbar	Sensitivity, dislike of interference
A	Endstroke short of baseline	Ambition
A	Balanced crossbar	Balanced personality
a	Top stroke extended to right	Over-effusiveness to cover up inherent shyness

Square	Mechanical skill, constructive ability
Crossbar rounded and rising	An entertainer
Wavy crossbar	Sense of humour and fun
Enrolled starting stroke	Shrewdness, opportunism
Crossbar looped in centre	Protectiveness, pity for the weakness of others

a

Printed letter	Artistic ability
Closed	Honesty, reserve
Open to right	Emotional honesty, talkativeness

a	Open to left	Tendency to talk about others behind their backs
a	Broad and open	Extreme talkativeness
a	Open at baseline	Hypocrisy, dishonesty
a	Knotted on left	Deceives others
a	Knotted on right	Deceives himself
a	Double knots	Deceives himself and others
a	Narrow and knotted	Secretiveness, reserve
a	Double narrow knots	Tendency to tell white lies
a	Open with knots	Talkativeness, untruthfulness
a	Ink-filled	Sensuality

	Square	Mechanical skill, constructive ability
	Hook inside oval	A gross deceiver
	Sharp angle at base	Hidden greed
	Endstroke rising to left	Self-protectiveness, introversion
	Long starting stroke	Caution; thinks before speaking
	Long endstroke	Warmth, generosity
	Very long endstroke	Extravagance, definite ideas
	Hook suspended inside oval	Over-concern with sex
	Club-like endstroke	Brutality
	Weak, descending endstroke	Timidity

a	Endstroke rising	A day-dreamer
a	Endstroke descending, with pressure	Obstinacy
q	Endstroke descending vertically	Strong likes and dislikes
a	Lasso-like endstroke	Sensitivity, love of poetry
a	Arcade endstroke	Matter-of-factness, lack of enthusiasm
a	Covering starting stroke	Misrepresentation of self
a	Endstroke rising into U/Z and curled	Pretentiousness
a	Broad	Imagination in a practical science; broadmindedness
a	Open at top	Love of fresh air, talkativeness, sincerity

B

B	Wide lower section	Gullibility
B	Narrow lower section	Scepticism, caution
B	Narrow	Shyness, inhibition
B	Tall first stroke	Enterprise
B	Very wide loop on first stroke	Inflated ego, a bluffer
B	Lower section inflated, with extended endstroke	Sense of one's own importance
B	Circle on endstroke	Concealment, egoism
B	Over-enriched	Vulgar taste
B	Upper section inflated on falling letter	Gains upper hand by intimidation

B	Starting and endstroke extended to left	Determination, desire to see things through to finish
	Long starting stroke	Needs a prop
	Very large, more than three times the height of small letters	Conceit, arrogance
	Small, not more than twice the size of small letters	Timidity, lack of self-esteem
	Wavy starting stroke	Sense of humour and fun
	Angular lower section	Resentment, insistence on having one's own way
	Hook to left	Avarice, greed
	Arc to left	Reluctance to accept responsibility
	Like figure 13	Mind for facts and figures
	Open at base	Talkativeness

Square	Mechanical skill, constructive ability
Unusual shapes	Erotic dreams and imagination
Large opening at baseline	Desire for self-knowledge
Very angular	Temper, cruelty

b

Wide upper loop	Expressive imagination
Narrow upper loop	Inarticulate, reticent
Like figure 6	Mind for facts and figures
Without upper loop	Taste, intelligence

Very open	Gullibility
Tightly closed	Caution, business ability
Sharply pointed upper loop	Penetrating mind, resentment
Amended	Hypochondria, neurotic tendencies
Tick at baseline	Persistence
Rounded starting stroke	Vivacity and chattiness
Tick starting stroke	Obstinacy
Wavy starting stroke	Sense of humour and fun
Looped first stroke	Pride
Looped endstroke	Imagination

	Rounded, open starting stroke	Talkativeness, sense of humour
	Long starting stroke	Fussiness, slow starter
	Long, straight starting stroke from below baseline	Resentment, argumentativeness
	Short, full upper loop	Desire to talk about oneself
	Tall, narrow, upper loop	Idealism, religious feelings
	Looped endstroke	Imagination
	Pointed at base	Uncompromising nature
	Bent starting stroke	Sensitivity, touchiness
	Enrolled	Egoism, greed
	Starting stroke from right	Pride, sensitivity

Ink-filled loop	Sensuality
Open at baseline	Hypocrisy, dishonesty
Without loop, and with endstroke to right	Austerity
Small circle on starting stroke	Jealousy towards one person
Large circle on starting stroke	Jealousy towards many people

C

Narrow	Shyness, reserve
Very rounded	Gentleness
Angular	Highly developed intellect

	Concave	Constructive mind, forward vision
	Ink-filled	Sensuality
	Rounded and very full	Idealism, kindness
	Square	Mechanical skill, constructive ability
	Enrolled	Shrewdness, opportunism
	Enrolled at base	Egoism
	Enrolled, with starting stroke	Calculating mind
	Enrolled, with long starting stroke from below baseline	Calculating mind, resentment
	Like a bracket	Capable of using force, if necessary, to control others
	Tick starting stroke	Quick thinker with strong judgements

Enrolled top and bottom		Craftiness, deceit
Claw to left		Avarice, greed
Starting with spot		Enjoyment of material success, preoccupation with the past
Endstroke extended under whole word		Self-admiration
Angle at base		Resentment, insistence on having one's own way
Pointed top and bottom		Penetrating mind, resentment, wilfulness
Tall first stroke		Enterprise
Unusual shape		Erotic dreams and imagination
Over-enriched		Vulgar taste
Loop at top		Vanity

Very large and enriched   Delusions of grandeur

C

Tick on starting stroke   Petulance, irritability

Narrow   Shyness, reserve

Angular   Quick mind

Angular, with pressure   Sharpness, temper

Rounded   Gentleness

Pointed at top   Penetrating mind

Enrolled   Shrewdness,
                                 opportunism

℮	Starting with spot	Enjoyment of material success, preoccupation with the past
(	Simplified	Simple, straightforward
Ⅽ	Square	Mechanical skill, constructive ability
e	Like letter e	Egoism
Ⅽ	Starting with closed loop	Business ability
C	Stroke extended under whole word	Self-admiration
Ⅽ	Loop on top	Vanity
e	Starting stroke through letter	Calculating mind
c	Ink-filled	Sensuality
C	Almost closed	Defensiveness

| | Angle at base | Resentment, insistence on having one's own way |

| | Endstroke rising to left | Introversion, self-protectiveness |

D

| | Open at top | Sincerity, talkativeness |

| | Wide open at top | Talks without thought of consequences |

| | Closed | Secretiveness |

| | Open at baseline | A gossip; loves to talk |

| | Large opening at baseline | Desire for self-knowledge |

| | Closed, with large loop | Caution, reserve |

	Claw on endstroke	Avarice, greed
	Looped, with rising endstroke	A flirt
	Looped, with long, rising endstroke	A day-dreamer
	Two separate strokes	Individualism, lack of adjustment
	Enrolled	Egoism, greed
	Endstroke extended to left	Sense of one's own importance
	Over-enriched	Vulgar taste
	Very broad	Vanity
	Diagonal rising endstroke	Ambition
	Tall first stroke	Enterprise

	Extended starting and endstroke	Good powers of concentration
	Unusual shape	Erotic dreams and imagination
	With starting stroke	Impatience, irritability
	Hook on starting stroke	Less self-assurance than outwardly apparent; stubbornness
	Long starting stroke from below baseline	Quarrelsomeness, resentment
	Slightly heart-shaped	Romantic nature
	Small, not more than twice the height of small letters	Timidity, lack of self-esteem
	Very large, more than three times the height of small letters	Pride, exaggerated love of luxury
	Very angular	Hardness, cruelty
	Very angular, with heavy pressure	Extreme cruelty, brutality

d

d	Tall U/Z	Integrity, idealism
d	Short U/Z	Humility, independence
∂	Greek-form	Love of culture, imagination
ϭ	Reversed letter 'd'	Rebelliousness
d	Open at baseline	Hypocrisy
d	Endstroke descending below baseline	Stubbornness, bad temper
♪	Like musical notes	Musical interest or ability, creativity
d	Looped endstroke	Self-protectiveness
d	Lasso loop	Interest in poetry, childlike personality

d	Wide loop	Sensitivity, vanity
d	Very wide loop	Open-mindedness, over-emotional tendencies
d	Very tall, wide loop	Over-emotional nature, love of singing
d	Narrow loop	Emotional repression
d	Square top to loop	Rigidity, aggression
d	Straddled	Taciturnity, quietness
d	Amended	Hypochondria, neurotic tendencies
d	Closed	Secretiveness
d	Open	Talkativeness
d	Stem pointed at top and base	Wilfulness, resentment

dark	Short stem, with small M/Z	Shrewdness
d	Ink-filled	Sensuality
d	Covering stroke on stem	A listener
d	Knot on stem	Extreme secretiveness
d	Knotted	Self-deception
od	Hook on starting stroke	Selfishness, possessiveness
d	Long starting stroke from below baseline	Resentment, quarrelsomeness
d	Endstroke curled under to left	Self-centredness, selfishness

E

Ɛ	Greek form	Love of culture
Ɛ	Enrolled	Egoism, greed
Ɛ	Enriched	Generosity, idealism
Ɛ	Over-enriched	Vulgar taste
End	Endstroke extended under whole word	Self-admiration
E	Narrow	Shyness, reserve
E	Amended	Hypochondria, neurotic tendencies
Ɛ	Two full arcs	Very quick mind
Ɛ	Two arcs	Good powers of observation

	Hook on starting stroke	Avarice, greed
	Starting stroke touching loop	Difficulty in mastering one's own affairs
	Long starting stroke from below baseline	Resentment, quarrelsomeness
	Angular	Cleverness, cruelty
	Extended middle stroke	Caution
	Short starting stroke, with loop	Dress sense
	Unusual shape	Erotic dreams and imagination
	Distorted	Sensitivity, touchiness
	Tick starting stroke	Impatience, irritability
	Heavy pressure on baseline	Physical energy

Ɛ	Endstroke curled under to left	Self-centredness, selfishness
Ɛ	Wavy starting stroke	Sense of humour and fun
Ɛ	Very angular, with heavy pressure	Cruelty, brutality

e

e	Ink-filled	Sensuality
ι	Like letter i	Keen mind, secretiveness
e	Broad	Loves to talk
ε	Greek form	Love of culture, refinement
e	Endstroke rising	Courage

Endstroke rising to left	Self-protectiveness, introversion
High-rising endstroke	A day-dreamer, a visionary
Whip-like	A sadist
Garland endstroke	Casualness, friendliness
Without endstroke	Caution; retiring nature
Short endstroke	Dislike of attention
Long endstroke	Generosity, consideration
Endstroke curling under to left	Self-centredness, selfishness
Endstroke descending to right	Reserve, timidity
Long, descending endstroke below baseline	Obstinacy, temper

ʃ	Endstroke descending vertically	Strong likes and dislikes
℮	Endstroke with upturned hook	Tenacity, outspokenness
℮	Endstroke with downturned hook	Dislike of criticism, contrariness
℮	Endstroke short and curved	Consideration
℮	Endstroke with heavy pressure	Brutality
℮	Snake-like endstroke	Slyness
℮	Long and curved endstroke	Friendliness, warmth
℮	Endstroke extended along baseline	Curiosity, suspicious nature
℮	Lasso-like endstroke	Sensitivity, love of poetry
℮	Endstroke turned downwards	Matter-of-factness, lack of enthusiasm

	Looped endstroke	Selfishness
	Endstroke rising and curved downwards	A show-off
	Endstroke extending over whole letter in semi-circle	Distortion of the facts
	Endstroke falling below baseline, with tick	Temper, irritability
	Angular	Calculating mind

F

	Top bar extended over whole word	Protectiveness, tendency to patronize
	Wavy	Sense of humour and fun
	Narrow	Reserve, shyness

	Angular	Cruelty, hardness
	Very angular, with heavy pressure	Extreme cruelty, brutality
	Over-enriched	Vulgar taste
	Cruciform	Religious leanings, fatalism
	Hook on starting stroke	Avarice, greed
	Tall first stroke	Enterprise
	Extended middle stroke	Caution
	Amended	Hypochondria, neurotic tendencies
	Long starting stroke from below baseline	Resentment, quarrelsomeness
	Simplified	Quick mind, austere taste

Very long top bar	Dreams of future success
Wavy top bar above stem	Egoist, show-off
Downward hook on right	Matter-of-factness, tenacity
Upward hook on right	Greed, envy
Upward hook on left	Dry humour, down-to-earth personality
Downward hook on left	Unwillingness to share
Whip-like top bar	A practical joker
Club-like, down-pointing top bar	Unkindness, cruelty
Rising top bar	Desire for self-improvement
Top bar extended, with heavy pressure	Domineering personality

f

Very wide upper loop	Over-emotional nature
Full upper loop	Articulate, open-minded
Narrow upper loop	Emotional repression
Short, full lower loop	Appreciation of good food
Knotted, with loop to left	Pride in self or family
Pointed upper and lower loops	Penetrating mind, resentment
Lower loop angular at base	Unwillingness to compromise, resentment
Triangular lower loop, with horizontal endstroke	Selfishness; a domestic tyrant
Simplified	Intelligence, quick mind

	Webbed foot	Will take advantage of his closest friends, who will never believe him capable of doing so
	Cruciform	Religious leanings, fatalism
	Wavy cross-bar	Sense of humour and fun
	Tick starting stroke, no upper loop	A clever observer of people
	Upper and lower loops in balance, M/Z very small	Under strain or pressure in daily life
	Knotted	Secretiveness, toughness
	Very long L/Z	Down-to-earth personality, love of outdoor sports, restless sexuality
	Short L/Z	Physical weakness, lack of energy
	Return stroke to left	Quick mind, fluency of thought, ability to take short cuts
	Ink-filled	Sensuality

	Balanced	Organized mind, managerial ability
	Large upper loop, no lower loop	Many ideas, with little follow-through
	Large lower loop, no upper loop	Practical, self-reliant person
	Unusual movements in L/Z	Unusual sexual interests (often found in the writing of homosexuals)

G

	Greek form	Culture, refinement
	Arc to left	Avoidance of responsibility
	Hook to left	Avarice, greed
	Looped starting stroke	Muddle-headedness

B	Unusual shape	Erotic dreams and imagination
G	Straight downstroke	Agile mind
G	Straight, short downstroke	Ambition, critical mind
S	Snake-like	Tendency to turn nasty under pressure
y	Wide open at top	Inability to keep a secret
g	Extra large lower loop	Inflated sexual imagination, materialism
g	Looped start, and hook on endstroke	Tendency to talk about others behind their backs
G	Heavy pressure on downstroke	Discontent, cruelty
g	Circle on starting stroke	Awkward; puts obstacles in the way of action
8	Hourglass	Awareness of time

	Wide open pendulum to left	Contemplation, poetic attitude to sensual world
	Enrolled endstroke to right	Egoism, greed
	Hook on endstroke	Self-love
	Like figure 9	Concentration, fatalism
	Completed figure 8 in L/Z	Unusual sexual interests, possible lesbianism
	Over-enriched	Vulgar taste ('naked lady on the tie' type)
	Wavy starting stroke	Sense of humour and fun
	Square	Mechanical skill, constructive ability

g

	Arc to left	Avoidance of responsibility
	Loop to left	Sexual vanity
	'Perfect love letter'	Warm and receptive nature; ability to enjoy a happy and fulfilling sexual relationship
	Endstroke rising	Initiative, optimism about sex or money
	Endstroke falling	Despondence about sex or money
	Endstroke to right	Altruism, sexual repression, sublimation of natural drives
	Endstroke curled to left	Clannishness
	Very narrow loop	Loneliness, sexual repression
	Hook to left	Avarice, greed

	Short, angled endstroke	Nervousness, sexual repression
	Straight downstroke	Fatalism, an inconsiderate sexual partner
	Long, heavy plunge into L/Z	Defensiveness, aggression
	Swinging endstroke, extended to left	Obsessional desire for constant change
	Long, straight endstroke to left	Indulgence in masturbation
	Unfinished narrow loop	Sexual weakness (possible fear of penetration)
	Low crossing	Sexual disappointment
	Corkscrew	Sexual inventiveness
	Small triangle in L/Z	Cold nature
	Large triangle in L/Z	A domestic tyrant, often caused by sexual or emotional disappointment

	Unusual movements in L/Z	Unusual sexual interests, (often found in the writing of homosexuals)
	Endstroke to right and returning to left	Kind intentions not fulfilled
	Short lower loop	Little energy or interest in sex
	Large lower loop, known as 'money bag'	Materialism, good sex drive and imagination
	Long or large L/Z	Love of outdoor sports, sexual restlessness
	Long, full L/Z	Easily becomes emotionally involved
	Covering stroke	Difficulty in giving, either financially or sexually
	Greek form	Love of culture
	Open to right	Appreciation of good food
	Small cradle	Sexual expectations unfulfilled

	Large cradle	Unresolved tie with mother figure
	Heavy pressure on downstroke, light return stroke	Good sex drive but weak follow-through
	Left-tending curve	Dependence on partner for sexual strength
	Very short, unlooped downstroke	Sublimation of sexual drive
	Downstroke ending in light pressure	Sexual energy initially strong but quickly dissipated; need for change of partner?
	Base of loop missing	Sexual disappointments in past; possible lower body weakness
	Spot at base of lower loop	Weakness or pain in ankle
	Spot slightly higher on lower loop	Weakness or pain in knee
	Hook on endstroke	Self-love
	Wide open pendulum	Poetic attitude to sensual world, contemplation

9	Very heavy pressure on downstroke	Violent temper, a passionate but thoughtless lover
g g	Completed figure 8 in L/Z	Unusual sexual interests, possible lesbianism
g g g	Some variety in loop formations	Easily stimulated sexually
g g g g g	A great deal of variety in loop formations	Lack of control
g g g	No variety in loop formations	Lack of sexual imagination
9	Like figure 9	Good judgement; mathematical ability

H

H	Narrow	Shyness, reserve
H	Broad	Broad-mindedness, extravagance

	Endstroke extended under whole word	Self-admiration
	Over-enriched	Vulgar taste
	Enriched, with added vertical stroke	Impudence, arrogance, a bluffer
	Very tall and narrow	Inhibition, shyness, pride
	Hooks to left	Avarice, greed
	Curved starting stroke	Opinionated
	Additional stroke before crossbar	Sensitivity, dislike of interference
	Like a gate	Impulsiveness, impatience
	Like letter N	Bluntness, directness
	Convex first downstroke	Obstinacy

	Upward hook on left of crossbar	Dry humour, down-to-earth personality
	Downward hook on left of crossbar	Unwillingness to share
	Convex downstrokes	Avoidance of responsibility
	Concave downstrokes	Tendency to sound people out for one's own advantage, deviousness
	Downward hook on right of crossbar	Craving for money and possessions
	Enriched but controlled	A strategist
	Angular, with pressure	Very bad temper
	Second downstroke taller	Enterprise
	Wavy crossbar	Sense of humour and fun
	Amended	Hypochondria, neurotic tendencies

| | Starting tick on falling letter | Impatience and irritability about small matters |

h

	Tall, rounded loop	Spiritual awareness, imagination
	Small loop at top of stem	A day-dreamer
	Short loop	Lack of imagination, humility
	Very wide loop	Sensitivity, over-emotional nature
	Very tall loop	Pride, idealism
	Ink-filled loop	Sensuality
	Endstroke to left	Unwillingness to compromise

ん	Well rounded loop	Thoroughness, balanced emotions
ん	Without loop	Good judgement, head ruling the heart
ん	Rounded M/Z	Gentleness, enjoyment of simple things
ん	Angular	Aggression
ん	Tall U/Z, without loop	Uncluttered thinking, lack of sentiment
ん	Square top to loop	Rigidity, obstinacy
ん	Snake-like middle zone	Wavering opinions
ん	Crook top to right	Pleasure-loving nature
ん	Crook top to left	Opinionated
ん	Very broad	A bluffer

Enrolled	Shrewdness, opportunism
Spot at top of loop	Possible eye-strain or headaches
Various breaks, or raggedness, in loops	Can indicate an organic or emotional ailment.
Endstroke descending below baseline	Stubbornness, argumentativeness
Endstroke short of baseline	Reluctance to admit having seen or heard anything
Wavy starting stroke	Sense of humour and fun
Long, straight starting stroke from below baseline	Resentment, quarrelsomeness
Small, rounded movement at top of stem	Spiritual unease
Downstroke of loop very faint	Reluctance to look back to the past
Upstroke of loop very faint	Reluctance to face the future

I

Small PPI of any type	Lack of confidence, poor self-image
Very tall PPI of any type	Self-confidence, pride in oneself
Any PPI made simply and in proportion to rest of script	Naturalness, willingness to co-operate with others
Single stroke	Straightforward, genuine nature, intelligence
'Consequential I'	High opinion of oneself, confidence, clear thinking
Any PPI made totally out of proportion to rest of script	Acting ability, fantasy, sometimes megalomania
Capital written as a small letter	Crushed, totally immature ego
Pound or dollar sign; like figure 7 or 9	Familiarity with figures, love of money
Unusual loops to left	Possible homosexuality

8	Closed	Over-concern with self
14	Like figure 4	Irritability, inability to see others' viewpoint
9	Reclining	Unfulfilled desires
ɔ	Unfinished starting and endstroke	Poorly developed ego, dislike of people generally
9	Over-inflated upper loop	Exaggerated sense of one's own importance
8	Small and cramped	Inferiority feelings, self-consciousness
9	Upper loop complete, endstroke short	Influenced by father
ɔ	Upper loop incomplete, endstroke extended to left	Influenced by mother
9	Very narrow upper loop	Timidity, reticence
9	Pointed at top	Penetrating mind

	Bowed back	Enjoyment of suffering at hands of loved one
	Like a flame	Disappointment, self-criticism, judgemental attitude
	Angular	Self-criticism, hostility
	Like a musical symbol	Musical interest or ability
	Descending below baseline	Deceit, subversiveness (often disregard for partner's feelings)
	Small top loop, curled endstroke	Vanity, hiding inferiority complex
	Written with lighter pressure than rest of script	Loss of identity
	Confused, involved in loops or angles	Self-consciousness, little sense of identity
	Small, curled up	Negation of the ego due to guilt feelings
	Curved, or ear-shaped	Tendency to take the easy way out, non-involvement (sometimes

found in the writing of
people with hearing
problems)

I I	Amended in any way	Ill-at-ease in present circumstances
I	Top and bottom strokes disconnected	Interest in ball games
J	Simplified, with curved base	Enjoyment of solitude, independence
J	Tall, with leftward hook at base	Pomposity
7	Simplified, with tick starting stroke	Clear mind, concise
J	Arc to left at base	Avoidance of responsibility
JJ	Enrolments	Egoism, greed
J	Endstroke rising to left	Contemplation
J	Lasso-like	Shrewdness, fixed ideas

	Small top loop, extended endstroke	Unwillingness to try anything new
	Artificial flourishes and loops	Lack of taste, mediocre mind, often with excessive vanity
	Very narrow	Repression, inhibition
	PPI written at a different angle from rest of script	Guilt complex
	Triangular base	Aggression
	Triangular base, with heavy pressure	Violent nature
	Balloon-like base	Imagination, fun-loving
	Cancelled-out upper loop	Self-hatred
	Like figure 2	Inability to relate intimately; feels second-class, either physically or emotionally
	Upper and lower loops ending to right	Tendency to blame others when things go wrong, limited insight

χ	Like letter X	Strong fears and dependence
ი	Arcaded	Self-protectiveness, need to be mothered

i

ι	Dot directly above	Precise, exacting nature
ι	Dot low and directly above	Capacity for detailed work, concentration, accuracy
ι·	Dot to right	Impulsiveness, intuition
·ι	Dot to left	Procrastination, caution
ι	Dot omitted	Carelessness, absent-mindedness
ι·	Dot high to right	Curiosity, impatience

ι	Dot very high	Lack of realism
ι	Dot very high, with light pressure	Spiritual awareness
ι	Dot low, with heavy pressure	Materialism, strong will, possible depression
ι	Arcade dot	Deceit, concealment
ι	Dot open to right, known as 'watching eye'	Good powers of observation
ι	Arc open to left	Sarcasm
ι *ι*	Dot like dash	Hasty temper, irritability
ι	Dot like arrowhead	Sharp wit
ι	Wavy dot	Sense of humour and fun
ι	Weak dot	Weak will, lack of energy

i (club-like dot)	Club-like dot	Sensuality, brutality
i (circle dot)	Circle dot	In female writing: desire for attention, eccentricity (often found in the writing of people who are good with their hands, perhaps in the field of design) In male writing: a feminine trait; interests are fashion, dancing, hairdressing, etc.
i (dot like vertical stroke)	Dot like vertical stroke	Critical nature, emphasis on principles
i (dot like tick)	Dot like tick	Ambition, desire for recognition
it (dot connected)	Dot connected to next letter	Clever combination of ideas
iiii (many dots)	Many different types of dot in same script	Inconsistent behaviour, good imagination, need for change and variety

J

4	U/Z like figure 4	Inability to see others' point of view
J	Enriched starting stroke	Awkward, fussy
2	Exaggerated L/Z loop to left	Musical interest or ability (possible homosexuality)
J	Angular at base	Temper, nervousness
J	Very sharp at base	Penetrating mind, resentment
J	Concave top bar	Desire to be the centre of attention
J	Like scales	Wavering in ideas and actions
June	Top bar extending over whole word	Protectiveness, tendency to patronize
J	Wavy top bar	Sense of humour and fun

	Starting stroke from right	Actor, show-off, limited insight
	Ticks both ends of top bar	Will use forceful means to control others
	Whip-like top bar, extended to right.	Will strive to control situations
	Top bar like horns	Obstinacy, tenacity
	Top bar waving to right	Egoism
	Top bar wavy on left	A practical joker
	Arc to left	Avoidance of responsibility
	Hook to left	Avarice, greed
	Top bar above stem	Deceit
	Cruciform	Religious interests, fatalism

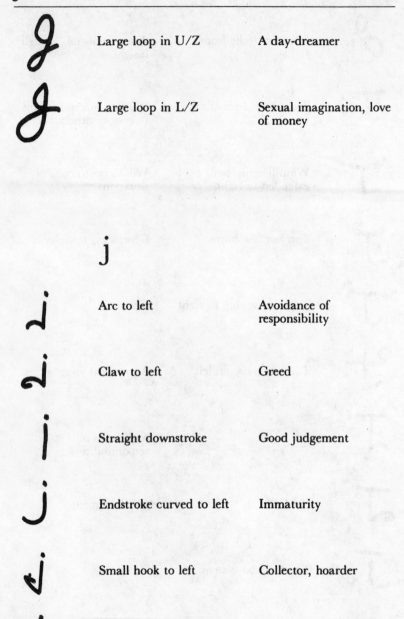

	Large loop in U/Z	A day-dreamer
	Large loop in L/Z	Sexual imagination, love of money

j

	Arc to left	Avoidance of responsibility
	Claw to left	Greed
	Straight downstroke	Good judgement
	Endstroke curved to left	Immaturity
	Small hook to left	Collector, hoarder
	Small tick to left	Aggression, nervousness

✓	Very long downstroke, with tick	Decisive, quick tempered
	Large loop	Egoist, show off
	Very small loop	Lack of energy and vitality
	Endstroke incurving	Sensitivity, some eccentricity
	Endstroke long and rounded to left	Impressionability
	Endstroke to right	Quick, active mind, altruism
	Cruciform	Religious interests, fatalism
	Knotted	Thoroughness, determination
	Dot omitted	Carelessness, absent-mindedness
	Dot to right	Impulsiveness, intuition

ɟ	Dot high to right	Curiosity, impatience
ɟ	Dot to left	Procrastination, caution
ɟ	Dot low and directly above	Capacity for detailed work, concentration, accuracy
ɟ	Dot open to right, known as 'watching eye'	Good powers of observation
ɟ	Heavy and thick dot	Strong will
ɟ	Weak dot	Weak will, lack of energy
ɟ	Wavy dot	Sense of humour and fun
ɟ	Arcade dot	Deceit, concealment

K

K   Endstroke extended   Self-admiration
under whole word

	Endstroke descending below baseline	Defensiveness
	Endstroke short of baseline	Ambition
	Loop to left of first stroke	Pride in achievements
	Angular and knotted	Efficiency, thoroughness, caution
	Like letter R	Eccentricity
	Separate strokes	Individualism, lack of adjustment
	Point through first stroke	Resentment of the opposite sex
	'Love knot'	Liking for people and sex

K	Endstroke descending vertically below baseline	Bluntness, uncompromising attitude
K	Three separate strokes	Many ideas, poor organizer
K	Tall first stroke	Enterprise
K	Concave second stroke	Desire to control others
IS	Snake-like second stroke	Moodiness, changeability
K	Bent first stroke	Back ailment or weakness
K	Curved starting stroke	Opinionated
K	Small rounded movement at top of first stroke	Spiritual unease
K	Over-enriched	Vulgar taste

k

Over-inflated loop to right	Rebelliousness, defiance
Tall first stroke	Enterprise
Tall upper loop	Pride, idealism
Small, rounded movement at top of first stroke	Spiritual unease
Broken upper loop	Possible organic problem
Spot at top of upper loop	Possible eye-strain or headaches
Upstroke of upper loop very faint	Reluctance to face the future
Downstroke of upper loop very faint	Reluctance to look back to the past
Various breaks, or raggedness, in loops	Can indicate an organic or emotional ailment.

	Angular and knotted	Efficiency, thoroughness, caution
	Endstroke extending under whole word	Self-admiration
	Narrow	Inhibition, emotional repression
	Very wide upper loop	Sensitivity, over-emotional nature
	Capital in middle of word	Eccentricity, tendency to get priorities wrong
	Endstroke descending below baseline	Defensiveness
	Crook top to right	Pleasure-loving nature
	Tick starting stroke	Obstinacy, determination
	Endstroke encirled	Egoism, self-love
	Amended	Hypochondria, neurotic tendencies

	Long, straight starting stroke from below baseline	Resentment, quarrelsomeness
	Starting stroke from right	Sense of humour, chatterbox
	Endstroke descending below baseline and to left	Dislike of compromise, argumentativeness

L

	Very large upper loop	Expansiveness, generosity
	Very large loop to left	Vanity, good dress sense
	Without lower loop	Secretiveness, shyness
	No upper loop	Positive attitude, materialism
	Enrolled	Egoism, greed

	Hook on starting stroke	Avarice, materialism
	Endstroke encircled	Egoism, self-love
	Over-enriched	Vulgar taste
	Endstroke extended under whole word	Self-admiration
	Full, but simplified	Taste
	Small loop at top of stem	Jealousy towards one person
	Small rounded movement at top of stem	Spiritual unease
	Without upper loop, endstroke encircled	Insincerity, greed
	Pound or dollar sign	Familiarity with figures, love of money
	Very narrow	Shyness, reserve

𝓩	Wavy starting stroke	Sense of humour and fun
𝓵	Starting stroke from right	Actor, show-off
𝗭	Curled starting stroke	Vivacity, chattiness
2	Like figure 2	Inability to relate intimately; feels second-class, either physically or emotionally

1

𝓵	Very tall loop	Pride, idealism
𝓵	Tall, full loop	Sensitivity, over-emotional nature
𝓵	Very broad loop	Broad-mindedness, imagination
𝗹	Without loop	Good judgement, self-confidence

ℓ	Narrow loop	Inhibition, emotional repression
L	Downstroke covering upstroke	Narrow-mindedness, secretiveness
e	Very short U/Z	Low aspirations
ℓ	Square top to loop	Obstinacy
e	Very small loop	Timidity
ℓ ℓ ℓ	Various breaks, or raggedness, in loops	Can indicate an organic or emotional ailment.
ℓ	Long, straight, starting stroke from below baseline	Resentment, quarrelsomeness
ℓ	Amended	Hypochondria, neurotic tendencies
ℓ	Point on loop and at base	Penetrating mind, insistence on getting one's own way
ℓ	Simplified	Quick mind, good grasp of essentials

	Pointed at base	Uncompromising nature
	Ink-filled	Sensuality
	No starting or end-stroke, large upper loop	Predominance of intellectual interests
	Hook on starting stroke	Acquisitive, a hoarder
	Long endstroke	Generosity, kindness
	Stunted endstroke	Meanness
	Over-extended endstroke	Caution; keeps people at a distance
	High-rising endstroke	Search for knowledge, occult interests
	Endstroke descending vertically below baseline	Bluntness, uncompromising attitude
	Spot at top of loop	Possible eye-strain or headaches

| | Downstroke of loop very faint | Reluctance to look back to the past |
| | Upstroke of loop very faint | Reluctance to face the future |

M

	Very broad	Extravagance, wastefulness
	Narrow	Shyness, inhibition
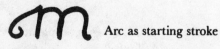	Arc as starting stroke	Speech-maker, actor
	First hump very tall	Very high opinion of oneself
	Descending humps	Aristocratic feelings, condescension
	Tall second hump	Dependence on others' opinion, self-consciousness, ambition

	Three loops	Attention seeker, pseudo-charm
	Arcades	Tact
	Like musical notes	Musical interest or ability
	Endstroke descending below baseline	Stubbornness, bad temper
	Large loop within first hump	Professional jealousy
	Small loop to left	Jealousy, possessiveness
	First stroke starting from right	Talkativeness, sense of humour
	Over-enriched	Vulgar taste
	Middle stroke lower	Social dissatisfaction
	Middle stroke higher	Ambition, ruthlessness

	Very wavy	Changeability, diplomacy
	Thread	Difficulty in making decisions
	Endstroke to left	Defensiveness
	Angular	Impatience, penetrating mind
	Garland	Warmth, softness
	Square	Mechanical skill, constructive ability
	Claw on starting or endstroke	Egoism, greed
	Starting with spot at baseline	Enjoyment of material success; possible 'skeleton in cupboard'
	Hook on starting stroke at baseline	Less self-assurance than outwardly apparent, stubbornness
	Very full and round	Imagination

	Endstroke crossing to left through letter	Depression
	Covering strokes	Avoidance of limelight
	Hook on starting stroke	Selfishness
	Large and flourished starting stroke	Desire to present a false image of one's worth
	All humps uniform in height	Intelligence, taste
	Endstroke descending below baseline to left	Dislike of compromise, obstinacy
	Endstroke descending below baseline to right	Forward vision
	Broadly spaced	Presumptuousness
	Endstroke with heavy pressure	Brutality
	Changing angle	Lack of integration

ℳ	Unusual printed capital, with angles	Firmness, artistic ability
ℳ	Endstroke rising into U/Z	Relationships based on shared religious beliefs
ℿ	Modern, simplified	Aesthetic sense, love of form, line, shape
ℳ	Angular top with rounded base	Keen mind, gentle nature
ℳ	Angular top and base	Rigidity, hardness; lack of humour
ℳ	Curled, arcade starting stroke	Desire for responsibility without ability to handle it
ℳ	Middle stroke peaked	Rudeness, sharpness
ℳ	Looped centre	Desire to control others
ℳ	Tall starting stroke	Enterprise

m

Claw-like endstroke	Avarice, greed
Very broad and flattened	A bluffer
Narrow	Shyness, reserve
Like letter w	Superficial charm
With small starting stroke	Fussiness
Like musical notes	Musical interest or ability
Tall starting stroke	Egoism
Small circle on starting stroke	Jealousy
Thread	Indecision

ᴽ	Endstroke descending below baseline, with pressure	Brutality, stubbornness
ᵯ	Tall first hump	Pride, egoism
ᵯ	Tall second hump	Desire to be well thought of
ᵯ	Endstroke short of baseline	Reluctance to admit having seen or heard anything
ᵯ	High arcades	Musical and artistic ability, manual dexterity
ᵯ	Extra hump	Compulsive need to check and recheck
eee	Upper strokes looped	Clairvoyant ability
ᵯ	Lower strokes looped	Worries about others
ᵯ	Endstroke pointed	Critical nature, faultfinder
ᵯ	Rounded	Kindness, gentleness

	Looped starting stroke	Secret worrier
	Angle starting stroke	Underhand behaviour
	Tick on starting stroke	Temper, underhand behaviour
	Centre section short of baseline	Tactlessness
	Horizontal starting stroke	Dry humour
	Modern, simplified	Aesthetic sense, love of form, line, shape
	Wavy, high starting stroke	Opinionated
	Like letter u	Hypochondria
	Endstroke descending below baseline	Stubbornness, dislike of compromise
	Decreasing second hump	Secretiveness, diplomacy

	Full circle starting stroke	Extreme sensitivity
	Curled stroke in U/Z	Artistic, creative ability
	Endstroke to left	Self-defensiveness
	Arcade starting stroke	Carefulness
	Broadly spaced	Presumptuousness
	Endstroke descending below baseline to right	Forward vision
	Hook on starting or endstroke	Avarice, greed
	Like a crown	Desire to be a leader
	Looped centre	Desire to control others

N

N	Narrow	Inhibition, shyness
N	Endstroke extended upwards	Enterprise
N	Endstroke to left	Self-protectiveness
NN	Small circle on starting stroke	Jealousy towards one person
NN	Large circle on starting stroke	Jealousy towards many people
N	Endstroke to right and below baseline	Sulkiness, tiresome behaviour
N	Arcade	Tendency to look on the black side
N	Large starting loop on baseline	Possessive; always puts obstacles in the way
N	Endstroke turned inwards	Self-protectiveness

	Endstroke extending over whole word	Protectiveness, patronizing attitude
	Wavy starting stroke	Sense of humour and fun
	Horizontal starting stroke	Dry humour
	Tick on starting stroke	Irritability over minor setbacks
	Long garland starting stroke	Slowness in starting new tasks or making decisions
	Starting stroke from below baseline	Resentment, argumentativeness
	Hook on starting stroke	Acquisitive
	Hook on endstroke	Tenacity
	Starting stroke lower	Self-consciousness
	Balanced and wavy	Artistic, creative ability

	Starting with loop	Self-deprecation
	Endstroke descending below baseline to left	Inability to compromise, a fighter
	Unusual shape	Sexual demonstrativeness
	Tall, hooked starting stroke	Overbearing personality
	Changing angle	Lack of integration
	Like letter u	Kindness, friendliness
	Starting stroke with hook to left	Egoism, greed
	Like musical notes	Musical interest or ability
	Points on baseline	Insistence on getting one's own way

n

symbol	Small circle on starting stroke	Jealousy towards one person
symbol	Extremely broad	Wastefulness, extravagance
symbol	Narrow	Shyness, inhibition
symbol	Wavy endstroke	Versatility
symbol	Angular	Analytical mind
symbol	Second stroke higher	Immaturity
symbol	Looped	Worries about himself
symbol	Curled, arcade starting stroke	Desire for responsibility without ability to handle it
symbol	Endstroke pointed	Critical nature, fault-finder

𝓃	Rounded, tall	Pleasure in working with one's hands, gentle personality
𝓊	Like letter u	Charm, friendliness
⊓	Square	Mechanical skill, constructive ability
⌐	Endstroke short of baseline	Reluctance to admit having seen or heard anything, non-committal
𝓃	Hook on starting stroke	Acquisitive
𝓃	Endstroke with pressure	Brutality
𝟷𝟷	Broken strokes	Frugality, nervousness
𝓃	Like musical notes	Musical interest or ability
∼	Wavy line	Changeability, diplomacy
𝓃	Arc on starting stroke	Speechmaker, actor

	Endstroke descending below baseline to left	Inability to compromise
	Like letter x	Strong fears and dependence
	Lasso-like endstroke	Sensitivity, love of poetry

O

	Square	Mechanical skill, constructive ability
	Full and rounded	Imagination
	Full and broad	Generosity, broadmindedness, a show-off
	Amended	Hypochondria, neurotic tendencies
	Unusual shape	Erotic dreams and imagination

Very narrow	Shyness, reserve
Several circles	Feelings of isolation, vivid imagination
Open at baseline	Hypocrisy
Open at top	Sincerity, talkativeness
Pointed at base	Insistence on getting one's own way
Enrolled	Deceitfulness, egoism, secretiveness
Large knot	Lack of directness
High-flying endstroke	Quick mind
Like a broad letter I	Self-centredness
Double circle to left	Evasiveness, secretiveness

	Double circle to right	Extreme evasiveness
	Diagonal stroke across	Self-deception
	Like figure 6	Craving for money and possessions
	Straight downstroke	Sarcasm, caustic tongue
	Hooked starting stroke and looped endstroke	Takes advantage of his friends
	Starting stroke above oval	Vindictiveness
	Open, with small loop to right	Changeability, moodiness
	Teardrop	A bully who likes to be in control

O

Narrow	Secretiveness
Broad and full	Broad-mindedness, tolerance
Over-large and full	Emotional, jealous
Broad and flattened	Dices with death in spite of fears and phobias
Written from left to right, open on left	Tendency to talk about others behind their backs
Open on right	Tendency to speak one's mind openly
Like letter e	Laziness
Pretzel	Attempt to hide one's true nature from others
Ink-filled	Sensuality

	Open at baseline	Hypocrisy, dishonesty
	Open and looped to right	Inability to keep a secret
	Closed, with one knot	Discretion, secretiveness
	Double looped within	Lack of self-discipline, hypocrisy
	Loop within loop	Insincerity
	Knotted circle, with wider second loop	Evasiveness, secretiveness
	Diagonal stroke across	Self-deception
	Like an onion	Liar, cheat
	Closed	Reticence, ability to keep a secret
	Long starting stroke from right	Hidden greed

୪	Crossed at top like letter x	Unreliability, ruthlessness
୯	Open at top	Honesty, sincerity, talkativeness
δ	Curved up and back	Imagination
♦	Pear-shaped	Boredom, lack of interest
◖●◗	Like a cat's-eye	Unkindness, unpleasantness
⊖	Horizontal line across oval	Shrewdness, cleverness
U	Like a horseshoe	Desire to control others
▷	Like a spade	Forcefulness, uncompromising nature

P

℔	Two separate strokes	Individualism, lack of adjustment
P	Very tall	Pride, vanity
♌	Claw to left	Avarice, greed
⌐	Original shape	Creative ability
⊥	Endstroke to left	Reserve, discretion
⌐	Loop extended over whole word	Protectiveness, generosity
⊖	Very wide loop on first stroke	Inflated ego, a bluffer
⊕	Over-enriched	Vulgar taste
⊓	Square	Mechanical skill, constructive ability

	Loop to left	Pride in achievements
	Angled top and bottom	Rigidity, hardness, lack of humour
	Wavy starting stroke	Sense of humour and fun
	Starting from left and in two separate parts	Desire to be the centre of attention
	Equal loop both sides	Extreme self-interest
	Hook on starting and endstroke	Desire to control others
	Whip-like	Strong need to control others
	L/Z narrowing to a point	Tendency to criticize and belittle others
	Pretzel, with inflated loop	Sexual vanity
	Angular, with pressure	Aggression, passionate nature

P	Very small	Shyness, reserve
p		
þ	Tall starting stroke	Enterprise, stubbornness
)ᵖ	Two separate arcs	Constructive and creative ability
P	Retraced L/Z	Physical stamina and endurance
P	Open on baseline	Generosity, a spendthrift
P	Open at top	Talkativeness, friendliness
P	Long L/Z loop	Love of physical activity
P	L/Z narrowing to a point	Tendency to criticize and belittle others

	Loop on starting stroke	Imagination, argumentative nature
	Peak on starting stroke	Peaceful, sensitive nature
	Open on baseline, long L/Z loop	Unkindness, callousness
	Pointed in L/Z	Desire to draw attention to others' weaknesses
	Rounded and looped starting stroke	A bluffer
	Tall angle in U/Z	Argumentative, contentious nature
	Wide upper loop	Argues with emotion
	Simple and original	Artistic and musical ability
	Curled endstroke	Curiosity
	Small loop on endstroke	Commercial sense

105

	Like a parachute	Extreme self-protectiveness
	Enrolment, ending in a spot	Enjoyment of material success
	Small loop on endstroke to left	Quarrelsomeness

Q

	Pressure on horizontal stroke	Quarrelsomeness, brutality
	Narrow	Shyness, reserve
	Very broad	Broad-mindedness, love of travel
	Heavy pressure on downstroke	Vitality, energy
	Open at top	Talkativeness

	Open at baseline	Hypocrisy, dishonesty
	Extra loop	Secretiveness, tact
	Large knot	Pride in self or family
	Loop to left	Self-deception
	Square	Mechanical skill, constructive ability
	Amended	Hypochondria, neurotic tendencies
	Like figure 2	Inability to relate intimately; feels second-class, either physically or emotionally
	Without horizontal stroke	Carelessness, rebelliousness

q

Claw to left	Greed, selfishness
Heavy pressure on downstroke	Vitality, energy
Two separate arcs	Creative ability, imagination
Ink-filled	Sensuality
Open on left	Tendency to talk about others behind their backs
Double looped in M/Z	Talkativeness, untruthfulness
Enrolled	Deceitfulness, secretiveness
Square	Mechanical skill, constructive ability
Knot inside oval	Keeps his own counsel; secretive

𝑞	Triangular L/Z	Dislike of interference in one's affairs
𝑔	Arc to left	Avoidance of responsibility
𝑞	Open at baseline	Hypocrisy, dishonesty
𝑞	Very short L/Z	Physical weakness, lack of energy
𝑞	Extended endstroke	Self-admiration

R

R	Narrow	Shyness, reserve
R	Square	Mechanical skill, constructive ability
R	Tall upper loop	Ambition
R	Endstroke descending below baseline	Obstinacy, temper

109

	Tall first stroke	Enterprise
	Inflated upper loop	Kindness, friendliness
	Tall and narrow	Pride, shyness
	Tall and full	Egoism
	With centre loop and curled endstroke	Pride, pomposity
	Over-enriched	Vulgar taste
	Angular and knotted	Caution, efficiency, thoroughness
	Endstroke returning to left	Defensiveness
	Small circle on starting stroke	Jealousy towards one person
	Large circle on starting stroke	Jealousy towards many people

	Hook to left	Greed, selfishness
	Very wide loop on first stroke	A show-off
	Open at top	Talkativeness
	Two separate strokes and hooked	Insistence on having one's own way
	Very rounded and full	Very effective bluffer
	Very long starting stroke and extended loop	Desire to curb others' freedom
	Narrow; endstroke descending below baseline, with pressure	Insistence on controlling situations
	Open and broadly spaced	A veneer of integrity
	Loop extended over whole word	Generosity, protectiveness
	Wavy starting stroke	Sense of humour and fun

r

	Flattened top	Broad-mindedness, a handyman
	Square	Mechanical skill, manual dexterity
	Peak on first stroke	Curiosity, critical nature
	Double peaks	Manual dexterity, versatility
	Simple	Quick, active mind
	Pointed top	Perceptive, probing mind
	Stunted	Repression
	Looped top	A day-dreamer
	Knot on first stroke	Pleasure in singing to oneself

Like Greek letter e	Like Greek letter e	Artistic interest and appreciation
	Endstroke returning to left	Self-protectiveness
	Rounded and simple	Dullness, placidity
	Two loops	Vanity, prejudice
	Starting loop	Shyness, reserve
	Endstroke extended over top to left	Self-protectiveness, evasiveness
	Like musical notes	Musical appreciation or ability
	Snake-like	Deviousness
	Extended endstroke	Generosity, kindness
	Large loop on first stroke	Over-awareness of one's physical attractions

	Like letter v	Attempts to confuse others
	Like an anvil	Cynicism, cruelty
	Like figure 2	Mathematical mind, materialism
	Broad and balanced	Visual awareness, good dress sense

S

	Simplified	Culture, taste
	Over-enriched	Vulgar taste
	Claw on starting stroke	Greed, avarice
	Like a chess pawn	Enjoys humiliating others

Arc at baseline	Avoidance of responsibility
Pound or dollar sign	Love of money, greed
Rounded and simple	Easy-going nature, mental laziness
Enriched	Enjoyment of music, especially rhythm
Very tall and simplified	Imagination, originality
Hooked endstroke	Deceit
Extended end stroke	Enterprise
Angular	Aggression, determination
Angular, with hooks	Rigidity, persistence
Long, straight, starting stroke	Hardworking but resentful

	Endstroke turned inwards	Defensiveness
	Very narrow	Reserve, shyness
	Snake-like	Tricky, devious nature
	Enrolled	Shrewdness, opportunism
	Looped at baseline	Mental agility, diligence
	Tilting, with loop at base	Critical nature
	Like figure 8	Mathematical mind, materialism
	Extra loop to left	Expansiveness, outgoing nature
	Loop to left, and horizontal crossing	Clever concealment of malicious intentions

S

busy	'Silly s' rising into U/Z	Difficulty in attempting new tasks
	Enrolled	Shrewdness, opportunism
	Wide open at baseline	Expansiveness, gullibility
	Very narrow	Shyness, reserve
	Very broad and open	Broad-mindedness, a public speaker
	Closed, with loop at baseline	Caution
	Very sharp top	Critical nature, sharp tongue
	Long, straight, starting stroke from below baseline, angular top	Hardworking but resentful
	Horizontal endstroke	Hidden greed

	Closed	Secretiveness
	Tightly closed	Difficulty in communicating
	Claw on endstroke	Avarice, greed
	Angular	Aggression, determination
	Very rounded	Kindness, gentleness
	Like a horseshoe	Desire to control others
	Like a chess pawn	Enjoys humiliating others
	Very angular	Will use force to attain his goal
	Open, with loop at baseline	Tenacity, diligence
	Rounded top	Yielding nature

T

Top bar high and removed from stem	High aspirations, not always followed through
Top bar like horns	Stubbornness, obstinacy
Amended	Uncertainty, anxiety
Like letter X	Uncertainty, depression
Top bar equally rounded both sides	Desire for limelight
Angled, with extension to right	Will use pressure to attain his goal
Like scales	Wavering in ideas and actions
Top bar joined to next letter	Will weigh all pros and cons before taking action
Concave top bar joined to next letter	Pretence of kindness to gain others' confidence

119

Whip-like	Attempts to control others by harassment
Wedge-shaped	Always objecting and criticizing
Long stem with low, concave top bar	Self-indulgence, assumed idealism
Top bar extending over whole word	Protectiveness, tendency to patronize
Convex top bar	Protectiveness, good self-control
Tall and lean	Calmness
Tall and balanced	Pride
Over-enriched	Vulgar taste
Wavy top bar	Sense of humour and fun
Top bar hooked to right	Determination, greed

亡	Angled	Frustration
亡	Angled, with pressure	Bad temper, aggression, cruelty
↑	Very simplified	Clear mind, organizing ability
J	Gracefully ornate	Artistic flair
T	Top bar hooked both ends	Sulkiness, persistence
7	Top bar looped to left	Egoism
†	Cruciform	Religious leanings, fatalism
ɡ	Looped endstroke	A show-off
The	Convex top bar joined to next letter	Passive desire to be the centre of attraction
†	Falling to left	Little respect for others

	L/Z narrowing to a point	Critical nature
	Left-tending endstroke	Attachment to the past
	Down-pointing top bar, with heavy pressure	Brutality, aggression
	Like figure 2	Inability to relate intimately; feels second-class, either physically or emotionally
	Long, left-tending, looped endstroke	Dishonesty
	With cross	Compulsive need to check and recheck
	Top bar excessively long, with heavy pressure	Domineering

t

	Cross omitted	Carelessness, absent-mindedness

↳	Low cross to left of stem	Caution, procrastination
↳	Middle cross to left of stem	Caution, slowness
↳	High cross to left of stem	Desire to lead, but too hesitant
✝	Low cross through stem	Caution; attempts to overcome feelings of inferiority
✝	Middle cross through stem	Caution; takes responsibility with great conscientiousness
⊤	High cross on top of stem	Leadership qualities with caution; often a desire for the unattainable
ᴛ	Short, low cross to right of stem	Content with a subordinate position
ᴛ	Short, middle cross to right of stem	Enjoyment of limited responsibility; conventional
ᴛ	Short, high cross to right of stem	Ability to control within a limited range
ᴛ	Long, low cross to right of stem	Ability to take greater responsibility and to solve problems

123

t	Long, middle cross to right of stem	Readily takes responsibility
⌐	Long, high cross to right of stem	Leadership qualities and overall ability to control
ᵗ	Low, straight cross away from stem	Acceptance of challenge, some impatience
t	Middle, straight cross away from stem	Goal-mindedness, zeal, drive, speed and impatience
ᵗ	High, straight cross away from stem	Leadership qualities and need to control
k	Low cross rising away from stem to right	Likes to control; not always easy to get along with
t	Middle cross rising away from stem to right	Ambition to get ahead at all costs
ᶜ	High cross rising away from stem to right	Leadership qualities with high intelligence
t	Straight, short cross, with light pressure	Weak will
t	Straight, long cross with light pressure	Lack of self-confidence; is easily persuaded

ℒ	Down-pointing cross	Obstinacy, contrariness
ℒ	Steeply down-pointing cross	Tendency to be critical about others
ℓ	Cross down-pointing from top of stem	Callousness
t	Convex cross	Self-discipline
t	Concave cross	Self-indulgence
t	Wavy cross	A mimic
t	Cross with upturned hook to right	Tenacity, envy
t	Cross with upturned hook to left	Matter-of-factness, humour
✳	Star-shaped	Inability to take criticism
7	Like figure 7	Ruthlessness

Cross increases from thin to thick	Temper which escalates
Cross decreases from thick to thin	Temper which dissipates
Very heavy cross	Strong opinions, temper
Club-like down-pointing cross	Uncertain temper, cruelty
Stem descending below baseline	Opinionated, wilful
Straddled	Taciturnity, quietness
Narrow, with endstroke returning to left across stem	Sensitivity, disappointment
Loop on stem	Vanity, talkativeness
Long, detached cross rising to right	High aspirations, demanding nature
High cross, above top of stem	Lack of realism, a day-dreamer

✝	Cruciform	Religious interests, fatalism
	Leftward, angular endstroke	Exacting, persistent, obstinate nature
	Leftward, angular endstroke with heavy pressure	Indomitable character
	Knotted cross	Concentration, persistence
	Wavy cross	Sense of humour and fun
	Endstroke returning to left across stem	Self-protectiveness, jealousy
	Looped stem, with curved endstroke	Extreme sensitivity
	Double stem	Fearfulness, suspicion
	Double cross	Compulsive need to check and recheck; possible dual personality
	Bent stem	Neurotic tendencies; self-absorption

`ì`	High cross, flying away from stem to left	Weak will, aggression
`´ì`	Cross to left and away from stem	Tendency to start things one cannot finish
`σ`	Like letter o with flying cross	Persistence about personal wishes
`ℓ`	Curled cross	Over-compensation for personal errors
`ψ`	Cross like horns	Obstinacy, tenacity
`ν`	Cross from base of stem	A quick, ready liar
`ν`	Like letter v	A quick mind with ready answers; not always truthful
`+`	Cross with downstroke tick to right	Enjoys ridiculing others
`+`	Cross with downstroke tick to left	Deep grudges held
`ν`	Straight stem, with upward curving endstroke	Always objecting and criticizing

ⳍ	Angled to left	Unwillingness to accept responsibility
Ɛ	Bowed stem, like letter E	Pseudo-friendliness
⇂	Very simplified	Organizing ability, clear thinking
ⱦ	Straight cross through double t	Protectiveness, maternal instinct
ⱦ	Straight cross over top of double t	Domineering personality
↗	Tent-like, with flying cross	Disloyalty, unfaithfulness
ⱨ	Down-pointing endstroke	Pessimism, lack of initiative
ⱦ	Spread out stem	Laziness; a slow worker
ⱦⱦⱦ	Variety of crosses	Varying control and willpower, versatility

U

Angular	Determination, persistence
Wavy starting stroke	Sense of humour and fun
Retraced	Inability to express oneself easily
Lasso loop	Interest in poetry, childlike personality
Garland	Easy-going nature, friendliness
Wavy line	Diplomacy, versatility
Horseshoe	Tendency to limit and restrict others
Snake-like	Tricky, devious nature
Long, curved starting stroke from below baseline	Actor, poseur

ll	Looped	Affection, pseudo-charm
u	Straight starting stroke	Attachment to the past
u	Long, straight starting stroke from below baseline	Resentment, aggression
u	Very broad	Bizarre imagination
u	Narrow	Shyness, inhibition
u	Tall second stroke	Enterprise
u	Hooked starting stroke	Obstinacy
u	Hook on second stroke	Vindictiveness, meanness

u

~	Wavy line	Versatility, diplomacy
ⳑ	Tall second stroke	Enterprise
⌔	Lasso loop	Interest in poetry, childlike personality
⌣⌣	Garland	Easy-going nature, friendliness
⋃	Very deep garland	Handyman, craftsman
⋀	Very angular	Persistence, inflexibility
⌣⌣	Deep, broad garland	Tendency to dramatize
⌣⌣	Very broad	Bizarre imagination
U	Horseshoe	Tendency to limit and restrict others

	Looped	Affection, pseudo-charm
	Long, curved starting stroke	Sense of humour and fun
	Long, curved starting stroke from below baseline	Actor, poseur
	Open at baseline	Hypocrisy, dishonesty
	Snake-like	Tricky, devious nature
	Retraced	Inability to express oneself easily
	Square	Mechanical skill, constructive ability

V

	Hook on endstroke	Vindictiveness

	Extended endstroke	Enterprise
	High, rounded starting stroke	Agile mind
	Over-enriched	Vulgar taste
	Over-enriched, with diagonal crossing	Over-friendliness, fussiness, vulgarity
	Wavy starting stroke	Sense of humour and fun
	High, rounded endstroke	Pride
	Endstroke crossing to left through letter	Depression
	Simplified and angular	Clear, penetrating mind
	Balanced	Continuity of thought
	Square root	Self-centredness

	Seagull	Underhand behaviour, unkindness
	Rounded, like letter U	Kindness, gentleness
	Crossed on baseline, like letter X	Untrustworthiness
	Very sharp and narrow	Critical nature
	Snake-like	Deceit
	Endstroke extending over whole word	Protectiveness, altruism
	Arcade endstroke	Fear of involvement

V

| | Over-enriched | Vulgar taste |

	Simplified	Keen mind, intelligence
	Rounded, like letter u	Kindness, gentleness
	Extended endstroke	Enterprise
	Wavy starting stroke	Sense of humour and fun
	Very narrow	Shyness, reserve
	Endstroke returning to left	Self-protectiveness
	Horseshoe	Tendency to limit and restrict others
	Looped	Self-deception
	Crossed on baseline, like letter x	Untrustworthiness
	Very broad	Broad-mindedness, extravagance

	Broad, with endstroke rising to right	Courage, daring
	Heavy pressure on endstroke	Unkindness, cruelty
	Endstroke curling downwards	Calm, matter-of-fact nature
	Whip-like starting stroke	A practical joker
	Endstroke tall and rounded	Pride

W

	Extended endstroke	Enterprise
	Full, and rounded at baseline	Sensitivity, love of poetry
	Large, with tall endstroke	Ambition

137

	Large, looped endstroke	Immaturity, theatrical behaviour
	Long, straight starting stroke from below baseline	Resentment, aggression
	Angular	Clear, penetrating mind
	Crossed in centre	A show-off
	Endstroke looped over whole letter	Eccentricity in dress or décor
	Three loops	Vanity, pseudo-charm
	Curved, with angular centre	Love of beauty
	Wavy starting stroke	Sense of humour and fun
	Small loop on endstroke	Interest in poetry
	Starting and endstroke curved inwards	Tendency to live in the past

Endstroke curved inwards	Self-protectiveness
Endstroke crossing to left through letter	Depression
Hook on starting stroke	Avarice, greed
Over-enriched	Vulgar taste
Small circle on starting stroke	Jealousy towards one person
Large circle on starting stroke	Jealousy towards many people
Very tall first stroke	Intellectual arrogance, vanity
Very narrow	Shyness, inhibition
Hook on endstroke	Vindictiveness, meanness
Covering strokes	Opportunism

	Square root	Self-centredness
	Very tall starting stroke, low finish	Desire to undermine others' confidence
	Angular at top, rounded at base	Keen mind, gentle nature
	Very broad	Extravagance, wastefulness
	Unusual shape	Erotic dreams and imagination

W

	Angular	Analytical mind, head controls heart
	Small loop on endstroke	Interest in poetry
	Square	Mechanical skill, constructive ability

ᴗᴝ	Two separate strokes	Individualism, lack of adjustment
ᴗᴝ	Wavy starting stroke	Sense of humour and fun
ᴡ	Crossed in centre	A show-off
ᴡ	Square root	Self-centredness
ᴡ	Full, and rounded at baseline	Sensitivity, love of poetry
ℓℓℓ	Three loops	Pseudo-charm, vanity
ᴡ	Small loop in centre	A clever manipulator
ᴝ	Endstroke curved inwards	Self-protectiveness
ᴡ	Long starting stroke from below baseline	Resentment, aggression
W	Very narrow and angular	Defensiveness

141

Spot on starting stroke	Fear of starting anything new
Balanced and wavy	Artistic ability, skill in handicrafts
Hook on starting stroke	Acquisitive
Wavy line	Versatility
Hook on endstroke	Vindictiveness, meanness
Unusual shape	Erotic dreams and imagination

X

Two separate strokes	Individualism, talkativeness, lack of social adjustment
Second stroke descending below baseline, with pressure	Holds strong opinions; aggression

✗	First stroke taller	Enterprise
✗	Straight downstroke, with loop to left	Quick, agile mind
✗	Horseshoe first stroke	Progressive attitude
✗	Back to back	Mathematical interests
✗	Bow and arrow	Untrustworthiness
✗	First stroke to left, ending with pressure	Temper, anger directed towards the past
✗	Strokes overlapping	Clannishness
✗	Joining stroke on left	Mercenary attitude
✗	Written as figures	Materialism, grasping nature
✗	Claw to left	Egoism, greed

✗	Starting with spot at baseline	Enjoyment of material success; possible 'skeleton in cupboard'
✗	Endstroke underlining whole word	Self-admiration
✗	Knotted in centre	Toughness, thoroughness

X

✗	Like figure 4	Materialism, mathematical mind
)C	Two separated strokes	Individualism, talkativeness, lack of social adjustment
✗	Second stroke descending below baseline, with pressure	Holds strong opinions; aggression
✗	Strokes overlapping	Clannishness
∝	Straight downstroke, with loop to left	Quick, agile mind

	Long, straight first stroke from below baseline	Resentment, aggression
	Hooks on starting and endstroke	Obstinacy, hardness
	Claw to left	Egoism, greed
	Split strokes	Lack of adjustment, shrewdness
	Loop on endstroke	Cunning

Y

	Wide and looped	Plays for sympathy, with a pose of helplessness
	Two separate strokes	Illogical mind, unreasonable behaviour
	Like letter X in M/Z	Guilt feelings in daily life

Like letter X in L/Z	Self-destructive tendencies
Hour-glass	Awareness of time
Wide open pendulum to left	Contemplation, poetic attitude to sensual world
Enrolled endstroke to right	Egoism, greed
Hook on endstroke	Self-love
Like figure 7	Concentration, fatalism
Completed figure 8 in L/Z	Unusual sexual interests, possible lesbianism
Over-enriched	Vulgar taste
Wavy starting stroke	Sense of humour and fun
Square	Mechanical skill, constructive ability

Arc to left	Avoidance of responsibility
Hook to left	Avarice, greed
Unusual shape	Erotic dreams and imagination
Straight downstroke	Agile mind
Straight, short downstroke	Ambition, critical mind
Inflated lower loop	Inflated sexual imagination, materialism
Heavy pressure on downstroke	Discontent, cruelty
Circle on starting stroke	Contrariness, tendency to put obstacles in the way

y

Ч	Straight downstroke	Fatalism, an inconsiderate sexual partner
Ч	Long, heavy plunge into L/Z	Defensiveness, aggression
ひ	Swinging endstroke, extended to left	Obsessional desire for constant change
┘	Long, straight endstroke to left	Indulgence in masturbation
ʋ	Unfinished narrow loop	Sexual weakness (possible fear of penetration)
Ƴ	Like hay-fork	Will use pressure to attain his goals
℮	Wide and looped	Plays for sympathy, with a pose of helplessness
∪	Two separate strokes	Illogical mind, unreasonable behaviour
Ⴘ	Low crossing	Sexual disappointment

	Corkscrew in L/Z	Sexual inventiveness
	Small triangle in L/Z	Cold nature
	Large triangle in L/Z	A domestic tyrant, often caused by sexual or emotional disappointment
	Unusual movements in L/Z	Unusual sexual interests (often found in the writing of homosexuals)
	Endstroke to right and returning to left	Kind intentions not fulfilled
	Short lower loop	Little energy or interest in sex
	Large lower loop, known as 'money bag'	Materialism, good sex drive and imagination
	Long and large L/Z	Love of outdoor sports, sexual restlessness
	Long, full L/Z	Easily becomes emotionally involved
	Covering stroke	Difficulty in giving, either financially or sexually

149

8	Like figure 8	Gentleness, intuition
y	Small cradle	Sexual expectations unfulfilled
y	Large cradle	Unresolved tie with mother figure
y	Heavy pressure on downstroke, light return stroke	Good sex drive but weak follow-through
y	Left-tending curve	Dependence on partner for sexual strength
ч	Very short, unlooped downstroke	Sublimation of sexual drive
ч	Downstroke ending in light pressure	Sexual energy initially strong but quickly dissipated. Need for change of partner?
y	Base of loop missing	Sexual disappointment in past: possible lower body weakness
y	Spot at base of lower loop	Weakness or pain in ankle
y	Spot slightly higher on lower loop	Weakness or pain in knee

Hook on endstroke	Self-love
Wide open pendulum to left	Poetic attitude to sensual world, contemplation
Very heavy pressure on downstroke	Violent temper; a passionate but thoughtless lover
Completed figure 8 in L/Z	Unusual sexual interests, possible lesbianism
Some variety in loop formations	Easily stimulated sexually
A great deal of variety in loop formations	Lack of control
No variety in loop formations	Lack of sexual imagination
Arc to left	Avoidance of responsibility
Loop to left	Sexual vanity
Endstroke rising	Initiative, optimism about sex or money

	Endstroke falling	Despondency about sex or money
	Endstroke to right	Altruism, sexual repression, sublimation of natural drives
	Curled endstroke to left	Clannishness
	Very narrow loop	Loneliness, sexual repression
	Hook to left	Avarice, greed
	Short, pointed endstroke	Nervousness, sexual repression
	Second stroke taller than first	Ability to control others
	First stroke taller than second	Inability to control others
	Like figure 7	Good judgement, mathematical ability

Z

Zoo	Endstroke extended under whole word	Self-admiration
	Snake-like	Cunning, deviousness
	Curved endstroke	Pleasant, easy-going nature
	Endstroke falling below baseline, with pressure	Aggression, depression
	Endstroke falling below baseline	Defensiveness
	Loop on starting stroke	Pride
	Very large	Desire for status, a show-off
	Top bar high and removed from stem	High aspirations
	Top bar high, to left, and removed from stem	High aspirations, not always followed through

	Hooked endstroke	Egoism, greed
	Tick on starting and endstroke	Nervousness, uneasiness

Z

	Very rounded endstroke, extended to left	Emotional tie with mother figure
	Endstroke falling below baseline, with pressure	Aggression, depression
	Endstroke to left and looped	Unusual sexual interests
	Like figure 3	Materialism
	Endstroke returning to right	Altruism, kindness
	Rounded and balanced	Easy-going, gentle nature

Looped centre	Looped centre	Fixed ideas, determination
Unusual shape	Unusual shape	Erotic dreams and imagination
Long, straight starting stroke	Long, straight starting stroke, extended endstroke to left	Romantic nature; argumentative

Character Traits

Abrupt	Upright, with clipped endstrokes	**a**
Absent-minded	Missing diacritics; significant gaps between letters	
Accident-prone	*See* Clumsy	
Accurate	Accurate diacritics; small size; angular connections; letters carefully formed	
Acquisitive	*See* Greedy	
Adaptable	'g' formed like figure 8; 'm' and 'n' like 'w' and 'u'; even pressure; garland connections; small size; connected	
Administrative ability	Quick speed; high F/S; upright; good layout; clear spacing	
Adventurous	Large size; irregular; right slant; quick speed; broadness	
Aesthetic	Wide left margin; clear spacing; Greek form of 'e', 'd' and 'g'; pasty pressure	
Affected	*See* Artificial	
Affectionate	Right slant; pasty pressure; long L/Z; broadness; garland connections	
Aggressive	Quick speed; heavy pressure; angular connections; heavy t crosses; angles or triangles on L/Z loops	
Alert	Light pressure; quick speed; simplified	
Aloof	Upright; clear word and line spacing; arcade connections	
Altruistic	Right slant; garland connections; extended endstrokes; altruistic loops in L/Z	
Ambitious	Large size; quick speed; rising baseline; long L/Z; tall U/Z; large capitals; rising t crosses; right slant; angular connections	
Amiable	*See* Friendly	
Amorous	Right slant; pasty pressure; long L/Z	

159

Analytical	Upright; small size; simplified; leanness
Animal lover	Rounded loops in U/Z and L/Z; pasty; broadness
Anti-social	All letters disconnected; leftward tendencies in M/Z; varying pressure; angular connections; leanness
Ardent	*See* Passionate
Argumentative	Long, straight starting strokes beginning below baseline; heavy, down-pointing, t crosses; angular connections; most letters disconnected; hooks, ticks and knots
Arrogant	Large capitals; descending humps on capital 'M'; upright; arcades in U/Z; tall PPI
Articulate	Connected; sharp pressure; simplified; broadness; open 'o' and 'a'
Artificial	Left slant; large capitals; counter-strokes; signature different from rest of script; slow speed
Artistic	Pasty pressure; clear spacing; original letter forms; balanced margins; good layout; tall arcade connections
Ascetic	*See* Austere
Aspirations (high)	Light or medium pressure; tall U/Z; rising t crosses; rising baseline
Assertive	Very large capitals; quick speed; angular connections; regular; heavy pressure; firm t crosses; triangles in L/Z
Assured	*See* Confident
Astute	*See* Shrewd
Athletic	Long L/Z loops, or single strokes with firm pressure
Attention-seeking	Large size; large signature and PPI; large capitals; use of red ink

160

Audacious	*See* Daring
Austere	Upright; wide letter, word and line spacing; simplified; leanness
Bad-mannered	Irregular left margin; bad layout; illegible writing; erratic word spacing
Bad-tempered	Heavy or varying pressure; angles in L/Z; heavy t crosses and endstrokes; irregular baseline and script; varying size of M/Z letters
Balanced	Regular and rhythmic; straight baseline; balanced zones
Bashful	*See* Shy
Bawdy	Pasty, with some smeary strokes; very long L/Z; right slant; over-enriched capitals
Belligerent	Long, straight starting strokes; heavy pressure; heavy t crosses; triangles in L/Z loops; angular connections
Benevolent	Garland connections; light pressure; altruistic loops in L/Z; extended endstrokes; rounded loops in L/Z and U/Z
Bi-sexual	Writing contains three or four distinctly different L/Z formations
Bizarre	*See* Eccentric
Boastful	Large capitals; fullness; broadness; counter-strokes; large signature and PPI
Boisterous	Heavy pressure; rising baseline; right slant; large M/Z; rising t crosses; open 'a' and 'o'; firm, long L/Z loops
Bossy	Tall capitals; long, heavy t crosses at top of stem; triangular loops in L/Z; the second of double letters taller than the first; underlined signature
Brave	*See* Courageous

b

161

Brazen	Large size; vanity loops; very large PPI; flattened 'm'; very large capitals; angular connections
Brisk	Quick speed; no starting strokes; simplified
Broad-minded	*See* Tolerant
Brutal	Very heavy pressure; thick and clubbed t crosses; angular connections; slow speed; thick or clubbed endstrokes
Bullying	Heavy pressure; angular connections; heavy, high t crosses; heavy, extended roofing strokes; triangles in L/Z
Bumptious	Very large capitals; signature larger than rest of script; vanity loops; large PPI; much underlining
Business sense	Good layout; long, narrow L/Z loops; leanness in all zones; right slant or upright; wide line spacing; words sometimes connected; initials or Christian name and surname joined in signature; angular connections
Busybody	Enriched letter forms; words and lines close together; narrow margins; rightward tendencies

c

Calculating	Upright; slow speed; covering strokes; narrowness
Callous	Very angular, both in connections and letter forms; absence of loops; leanness
Calm	*See* Composed
Candid	*See* Frank
Capricious	Varying size of M/Z letters; mixed slant; varying pressure; concave t crosses; irregular; thread connections
Careful	Medium size; firm pressure; accurate diacritics; legible writing; closed 'o' and 'a'; signature similar to rest of script; balanced margins; slow speed

Careless	Inaccurate or omitted diacritics; varying pressure; illegible script; mingling
Cautious	Left slant; diacritics to left of stem; closed 'o' and 'a'; initial letter separated from rest of word; slow speed; arcade connections; address on envelope in lower left quarter
Changeable	*See* Volatile
Charming	Garland connections; rounded letter forms; right slant; extended endstrokes
Chatterbox	Uneven spacing between words and lines; mingling; right slant; open 'o' and 'a'; broadness; narrow margins
Childish	*See* Immature
Clairvoyant	*See* Psychic ability
Clear-thinking	Connected; clear word and line spacing; legible script; good layout
Clumsy	Mingling; ornate capitals; irregular
Cold	*See* Unfeeling
Comedian	Rising endstrokes; wavy t crosses and endstrokes; fairly disconnected; pasty; original letter forms
Common sense	Upright or slight right slant; regular; straight baseline; simplified; no loops in U/Z or L/Z; small or medium size; one or both loops omitted on 'f'
Communicative	Connected; right slant; open 'o' and 'a'; broadness; garland connections; narrow lower margins; capital 'B' open at base
Companionable	Garland and thread connections; letters decreasing in size at end of words; right slant
Compassionate	Generally loopy writing; fairly disconnected; right slant; garland connections
Competent	*See* Efficient

Competitive	Angular connections; large size; heavy pressure; closed 'o' and 'a'
Complacent	*See* Smug
Composed	Regular; rhythmic; upright; arcade connections; accurate diacritics; clear spacing
Compulsive	Small size; lateral pressure; tall U/Z; long L/Z; small M/Z; no endstrokes; regular, with too much uniformity; extremely connected
Conceited	Very large capitals; inflated U/Z loops; vanity loops; large PPI; triangles in L/Z loops; signature very large in relation to rest of script
Concentration (good powers of)	Small writing; connected; simplified; accurate, low i dots; short U/Z and L/Z
Conciliatory	Thread and garland connections; no angles; rhythmic; regular; flattened arcades; letters decreasing in size at end of words
Condescending	*See* Patronizing
Confident	Quick speed; large size; broadness; right slant or upright; rising lines; large PPI; firm pressure; no starting strokes; angular connections; underlined signature
Conformist	*See* Conventional
Conscientious	Straight baseline; accurate diacritics; connected; regular; tall U/Z; slow speed
Conservative	Good layout; clear spacing; regular; rhythmic; legible; right slant; arcade connections
Considerate	Good layout; clear spacing; straight left margin; regular; broadness; legible; right slant
Consistent	Regular size of M/Z letters; constantly even spacing; even pressure and consistent letter forms; balanced zones; medium size

Constructive	Original letter forms; clever linking between letters and words; square letter forms or all block capitals
Contemplative	*See* Meditative
Contented	Rhythmic; straight baselines; rounded loops; signature same as rest of script; small U/Z and L/Z with normal M/Z
Contentious	*See* Argumentative
Contradictory	Medium speed and F/S; variety of connections; inconsistent letter forms; mixed slant; slant of signature different from rest of script
Contrary	Reversed letters; counter-strokes; covering strokes; diacritics sometimes omitted
Controlled	*See* Self-disciplined
Conventional	Right slant; medium size; copybook form; consistently even margins; arcade connections
Co-operative	Rounded letter forms; legible; signature matching rest of script; right slant; garland connections; connected; 'g' like figure 8
Corrupt	This only applies when all the following signs are consistently present in the writing sample: M/Z ovals, e.g. 'a', 'o', 'b', 'd', open at baseline; covering strokes; counter-strokes; smeary writing; extreme pastiness; low F/S
Courageous	Firm or heavy pressure; firm t crosses; broadness; right slant; straight baseline; quick speed; large size
Courteous	Good layout; clear spacing; arcade connections; legible; straight left margin; endstrokes long and rising
Covetous	Crowded letters and words; no margins; short endstrokes; hooks on starting or endstrokes
Cowardly	Light pressure; weak t crosses; narrowness; wide right margin; endstroke of 'e' descending to right

Creative	Original letter forms; wide word and line spacing; 'g' like figure 8; fullness; fairly disconnected; arcade connections; pasty
Credulous	Capital 'B' with fuller lower section; broadness; small U/Z loops; open 'o' and 'a'
Criminal tendencies	Low F/S; very large or very small size; pronounced left or right slant; very heavy or sharp pressure; very broad or very narrow; angular; counter-strokes; covering strokes; double-walling; M/Z ovals open at baseline
Critical ability	Tent-shaped i dots; very angular connections; upright; wide word and line spacing; simplified; disconnected; leanness in all three zones
Crooked	*See* Criminal tendencies
Cruel	Heavy t crosses, thickening at ends or down-pointing; heavy pressure; endstrokes descending below baseline; angular connections; hooks like claws; triangles in L/Z
Cultured	Graceful letters and capitals; wide margins; well balanced spacing; Greek form of 'e', 'd' and 'g'; good layout
Cunning	Letters decreasing in size at end of words to illegible threads; 'a' and 'o' double-knotted at top
Curiosity	High i dots; pointed tops to M/Z letters; tall, pointed U/Z
Cynical	Upright; narrowness; leanness; down-pointing t crosses
d Daring	Large size; broadness; quick speed; firm pressure; t crosses to right of stem
Deceitful	Closed, looped 'a' and 'o'; irregular baseline; covering strokes; narrowness
Decisive	Long, straight downstrokes in L/Z; upright; leanness; some angular connections; no thread connections or starting strokes; firm t crosses

Dedicated	Connected; angular connections; simplified; firm pressure; diligence loops
Defeatist	Falling baseline; narrowness; weak pressure; left slant; low t crosses; small size; small PPI; starting strokes
Defenceless	*See* Vulnerable
Deferential	*See* Respectful
Defiant	Omitted diacritics; illegible; letters written in the reverse direction from normal
Deft	Quick speed; clear spacing; looped U/Z and L/Z; small size; distinct pressure; legible; good layout; tall first stroke on 'p'
Degenerate	*See* Depraved
Delegating (bad at)	Small size, particularly M/Z; some narrowness
Delusions (suffers from)	Artificial fullness in U/Z and L/Z
Demanding	Large M/Z; angular connections; no starting strokes; large PPI; firm t crosses; no loops in U/Z
Demonstrative	Right slant; pasty or heavy pressure; many flourishes; open 'a' and 'o'; garland connections; loops in U/Z and L/Z; extended endstrokes
Dependable	*See* Reliable
Dependent	Small size; low diacritics; left slant; connected
Depraved	Too much thread connection; varying size of M/Z letters; irregular baseline; very varying pressure; angular connections; triangles in L/Z; heavy t crosses; smeary strokes
Depressed	Falling baseline; varying pressure; drooping garlands; tendency to cancel out signature through M/Z letters; very wide right margin; address on envelope placed to left

Determined	Angular connections; firm t crosses; regular; heavy pressure; firm downstrokes in L/Z with no loops
Devious	Covering strokes; closed 'o' and 'a'; arcade connections; amended letters or figures; thread connections
Devoted	Rising baseline; small size; right slant; connected; roofing strokes
Devout	*See* Religious
Dextrous	*See* Deft
Diffident	Slow speed; light pressure; small capitals; small size; PPI small or like small 'i'; t crosses weak or to left of stem
Dilatory	*See* Procrastinating
Diligent	Diligence loops; some starting strokes; firm pressure; right slant; connected; some angular connections
Diplomatic	Letters decreasing in size at end of words; thread connections at end of words; closed 'o' and 'a'; arcade connections; balanced zones
Direct	No starting strokes; short endstrokes; simplified; t crosses to right of stem
Disappointed	Low crossing of L/Z loops; falling baseline; drooping garlands; clipped endstrokes
Disarming	Letters decreasing in size at end of words; thread endings; closed 'o' and 'a'; wavy line connections
Discerning	Disconnected; sharp pressure; leanness; points on M/Z letters and U/Z loops; wide spacing; upright
Disciplined	*See* Self-disciplined
Discontented	Arhythmic; irregular baseline; points on loops; varying size of M/Z letters; irregular spacing

Discreet	Letters decreasing in size at end of words; 'o' and 'a' closed; arcade connections; simplified
Discriminating	Distinct or sharp pressure; upright; fairly connected; simplified; clear spacing; some narrowness
Dishonest	Breaks in M/Z ovals at baseline; counter-strokes; closed and knotted 'o' and 'a'; irregular baseline; varying size of M/Z letters; covering strokes; double walling
Disillusioned	Falling lines; low crossing of L/Z loops; upright or left slant
Disloyal	Mingling; mixed slant; irregular baseline; open 'a' and 'o'
Disorganized	Poor layout; mingling; irregular; omitted diacritics; mixed slant; uneven spacing
Dissatisfied	*See* Discontented
Dissipated	Very pasty, with ink-filled M/Z letters; concave t crosses; thread connections; broken or trembling strokes; inability to complete a rounded movement
Distrustful	*See* Suspicious
Dogmatic	Angular connections; firm t crosses; rising lines; arcade connections; regular; accurate diacritics; sharp pressure
Domesticated	Medium size; accurate diacritics; pasty; loops on U/Z and L/Z
Domineering	Very tall capitals; heavy t crosses at top of stem; roofing strokes; heavy pressure; large size signature and PPI
Dramatizing	Long, full L/Z loops; deep garlands; some M/Z letters rising into U/Z; large, triangular L/Z
Dreamer	Full, exaggerated L/Z loops; left slant; light pressure; fullness in U/Z; high t crosses above stem

Dull	Very connected; rounded letters; copybook form; no variation in, or originality of, letter forms
Dynamic	Heavy pressure; angular connections; firm t crosses; large size; regular; signature large and strongly underlined
e Earthy	Heavy or pasty pressure; predominance of L/Z; large size
Easy going	*See* Relaxed
Easily influenced	Very garlanded connections; fluctuation of size in all zones; thread connections; broadness
Eccentric	Bizarre letter forms; illegible, involved signature; illegible script; irregular; large M/Z with small U/Z and L/Z; unusual ink colours
Economical	Narrow word and line spacing; narrow margins or no margins; short or clipped endstrokes; simplified; small size; narrowness
Educated	Good layout; Greek form of 'e', 'd' and 'g'; quick speed; block capitals; simplified; letters decreasing in size at end of words
Effeminate	Rounded movements; rather disconnected; light pressure; circle i dots; left slant; leftward tendencies in L/Z
Efficient	Quick speed; clear spacing between words and lines; legible; upright; arcade connections; single strokes in U/Z and L/Z
Effusive	Marked right slant; pseudo-garlands; open 'a' and 'o'; pasty; many flourishes
Egoist	Very large M/Z; very large capitals and signature; PPI disproportionately large; inflated U/Z loops; very broad or very narrow; leftward tendencies; disconnected
Elusive	Thread connections; mixed slant; irregular; varying pressure; variations in all three zones

Emotional	Irregular; large, full M/Z; marked right slant; pasty; inflated loops in U/Z and L/Z
Empathic	Right slant; disconnected, or fairly disconnected with garland connections
Energetic	Quick writing; regular and rhythmic; large; heavy pressure; firm downstrokes; long L/Z loops; angular connections; simplified; i dots as dashes to right of stem
Energy-lacking	*See* Listless
Enquiring mind	Tall, lean, pointed U/Z; high i dots; simplified; small size; quick speed; sharp points on M/Z letters
Enterprising	*See* Adventurous
Entertainer	Very large and inflated U/Z loops; wavy diacritics; large size; inflated PPI and signature
Enthusiastic	Quick speed; long, high t crosses to right of stem; rising baseline; heavy or medium pressure; right slant; narrow right margin; irregular; large size
Entrepreneur	Large size; upright or right slant; angular and thread connections; balanced zones; quick speed; broadness; large PPI; some disconnection; long, narrow L/Z loops; original letter forms
Envious	Left slant; heavy or uneven pressure; inward curving hooks on t crosses or endstrokes; heavily underlined signature; 'o' and 'a' larger in M/Z
Erratic	*See* Unpredictable
Erudite	*See* Learned
Ethical	High F/S; leanness in all zones; regular; tall U/Z; angular connections; straight baseline; legible script and signature
Evasive	Thread and wavy line connections; covering strokes; closed 'o' and 'a'; flattened arcades;

171

endstrokes of some letters not completed to
baseline

Even-tempered	Garland connections; straight baseline; upright or slight right slant; regular; rhythmic; balanced zones; even spacing
Exaggerates	Large writing with flourishes; broadness; very inflated U/Z and L/Z loops; right slant; extremely wide margins and word spacing; large capitals
Excitable	Marked right slant or mixed slant; high diacritics; varying pressure; long starting strokes; irregular; rising baseline
Exhibitionist	Very large size; very large capitals and signature; broadness; inflated capital 'D'; unusual ink colours
Explosive	Small, ink-filled M/Z letters 'a', 'o' or 'e'; heavy pressure; very connected; narrow letters and loops; thick, heavy t crosses; angles and triangles in L/Z loops
Extravagant	Very wide margins; large writing; wide spaces between words; irregular; predominant U/Z; broadness; extended endstrokes
Extravert	Right slant; large writing; broadness; quick speed; right-tending movements generally
Exuberant	Rising baseline; marked right slant; fullness in all three zones; garland connections; open 'o' and 'a'; diacritics to right of stem; pasty
f Fair-minded	Upright; balanced zones; straight baseline; regular
Faithful	Upright; even baseline; closed 'a' and 'o'; simplified; regular M/Z; perfectly formed 'g' with completed L/Z loop
Fanatic	Very angular connections; firm downstrokes; medium or large size; heavy pressure; heavy t crosses or cruciform 't's; capital letters written as two or more separated strokes

Far-sighted	Right slant; broadness; wide left margin; fairly disconnected; regular; U/Z and L/Z large in relation to M/Z; some angular connections
Fashion-conscious	*See* Trendy
Fastidious	Small size; light or lateral pressure; legible; good layout; accurate diacritics; slow speed
Fearless	Large size; heavy pressure; regular; right slant; broadness; firm t crosses; quick speed; no starting strokes; narrow margins
Feather-brained	Slow speed; many amended letters; copybook form; enriched capitals; mingling; open 'a' and 'o'; low F/S
Fervent	*See* Intense
Fierce	Heavy pressure; angular connections; angles or triangles in L/Z loops; heavy, thick t crosses
Flamboyant	Large size; large PPI; broadness; large, involved signature; tall, enriched capitals; fullness
Flatterer	Flattened arcades; thread connections; letters decreasing at end of words; broadness; endstrokes going up and left and ending in a dot
Flexible	*See* Adaptable
Flippant	Wavy t crosses; garland connections; medium or small size; irregular left margin; irregular script
Flirtatious	Rising, curled endstrokes to right; pasty; small L/Z loops; broadness
Forceful	*See* Dynamic
Forgetful	Large breaks inside words; letters or words omitted; diacritics sometimes missing; disconnected; right-tending movements in U/Z

173

Formal	Arcade connections; wide word and line spacing; upright; wide upper margin; enriched capitals
Forthright	Straight baseline; firm pressure; letters increasing in size at end of words; regular; no starting strokes; open 'a' and 'o'; broadness
Frank	Quick speed; open 'a' and 'o'; letters at end of words increasing in size; straight baseline; broadness; garland connections; signature same as rest of script; simplified
Friendly	Garland connections; right slant; rounded loops in L/Z; broadness; rounded letter forms; extended endstrokes; pasty
Frivolous	Markedly rising baseline; copybook form; flourishes and ornate letter forms; right slant; shallow garlands
Frugal	*See* Economical
Frustrated	Knotted 'o' and 'a'; varying pressure; signature encircled; points on U/Z and L/Z loops; narrowness; ticks on starting strokes
Fulfilled	*See* Contented
Fun-loving	Right slant; wide L/Z loops and high, wide U/Z loops; pasty; broadness; wavy t crosses
Fussy	Small size; accurate diacritics; i dots like dashes; regular; very legible; good layout; lateral pressure
g Gauche	Letters increasing in size at end of words; mingling or jostling of M/Z letters; involved PPI; some disconnection
Generous	Quick speed; right slant; long endstrokes; wide word spacing; large size; broadness; garland connections; enriched; wide left margin
Genial	Right slant; broadness; large size; dominant M/Z; extended endstrokes; capital 'M' with pointed tops

Gentle	Garland connections; 'm' and 'n' with rounded tops; light pressure
Genuine	Quick speed; simplified; signature same as rest of script; legible
Glib	Connected writing; open 'a', 'o' and 'd'; right slant; broadness; narrow lower margin; vanity loops; no starting strokes
Gluttonous	*See* Greedy
Go-getter	Large size; right slant; rising baseline and t crosses; rightward tendencies in L/Z loops; broadness; some angular connections; good layout; good horizontal tension; quick speed
Good-natured	Garland connections; regular; rhythmic; right slant; straight baseline; rounded loops; balanced zones; clear spacing
Gossip	Open 'a', 'o' and 'd'; connected; mingling; narrow word and line spacing; narrow margins
Graceful	Fullness in L/Z; good layout; rhythmic; even pressure; long, garlanded starting strokes
Gracious	Garland connections; rounded script; extended endstrokes; straight left margin; legible
Greedy	Crowded letters and words; narrow margins; short endstrokes; hooks on starting or endstrokes; inflated figures; pasty
Gregarious	Narrow right margin; right slant; words very close together; connected; large size
Guilt complex	Small size; drooping garlands; narrowness; block capitals throughout; amended script; amended or very reduced PPI
Gullible	*See* Credulous
Gushing	*See* Effusive
Handicrafts (good at)	Circle i dots; pasty; fairly disconnected; fullness

h

Hard-hearted	*See* Unfeeling
Hard-working	*See* Industrious
Harmonious	Fairly regular; rhythmic; rounded loops in U/Z and L/Z; garland connections; no angles
Headstrong	*See* Wilful
Heartless	*See* Unfeeling
Helpful	*See* Obliging
Henpecked	Small writing; flattened M/Z; weak pressure and weak t crosses; leftward tendencies in L/Z
Hesitant	Slow speed; t crosses to left of stem; varying pressure; wide right margin; starting strokes
High-minded	*See* Idealistic
High-spirited	*See* Exuberant
Highly-strung	Varying pressure; marked right or left slant; irregular baseline; irregular script; pointed U/Z and L/Z loops
Hoarder	Small, narrow writing; no margins; t crosses with upturned hook; hooks, ticks and knots
Honest	Quick speed; high F/S; right slant; simplified; closed 'a' and 'o'; very legible; signature same as rest of script; no covering strokes
Hospitable	High F/S; garland connections; right slant; endstrokes extended to right; large size; narrow margins
Humanitarian	*See* Altruistic
Humble	Small capitals; small size; simplified; small PPI; low t crosses
Humorous	Wavy t crosses; curved i dots; garland connections; broadness; pasty; original letter forms

Hypersensitive	Irregular; broad, with light pressure; leftward tendencies in PPI; left or mixed slant; looped, sharp t crosses
Hypochondriac	Amended letters; some narrowness
Hypocritical	Arcade connections; irregular baseline; slow speed; counter-strokes; covering strokes; illegible
Idealistic	Dominant U/Z; large size with irregular script; light pressure; rising endstrokes
Idle	*See* Lazy
Imaginative	Tall U/Z and long L/Z loops; t crosses above stem; high i dots; fullness; broadness; disconnected; tall, enriched capitals
Immature	Round, copybook forms; irregular; short, full U/Z loops; irregular spacing; dominant M/Z
Immoral	Pasty and/or smeary pressure; very long L/Z, often with inflated loops; small U/Z; mingling; mixed slant; concave t crosses; counter-strokes; irregular baseline
Impatient	Right slant; light pressure; quick speed; illegible; i dots like dashes; long, light t crosses to right of stem; diacritics often omitted; widening left margin
Impetuous	*See* Impulsive
Implacable	Angular connections; heavy t crosses; heavy pressure; no endstrokes; narrowness
Impressionable	Garland connections; varying height of U/Z loops
Impulsive	Quick speed; diacritics to right of stem; marked right slant; irregular; rising lines; words close together
Inaccurate	*See* Careless
Inarticulate	Tightly closed and knotted 'o' and 'a'; small size; arcade connections; points on loops; upright or left slant; narrowness; disconnected

i

Inconsiderate	Illegible script; uneven left margin; clipped endstrokes; illegible signature; dominant M/Z
Inconsistent	Mixed slant; thread connections; varying pressure; varying size of M/Z letters; irregular baseline; same letter written in different ways; block capitals in middle of word
Indecisive	Left or mixed slant; thread connections; weak t crosses; light pressure; diacritics to left of stem
Independent	Upright; straight baseline; tall, simplified capitals; some diacritics omitted; clear word spacing
Industrious	Firm pressure; some starting strokes; connected; right slant; regular; well-developed L/Z; quick speed; accurate diacritics; diligence loops
Inefficient	Slow speed; mingling; variation in word and line spacing; illegible; irregular; some diacritics omitted
Inflexible	Angular and arcade connections; narrowness; very regular; heavy pressure; firm t crosses; endstrokes descending to right; potlids
Ingenious	*See* Inventive
Inhibited	Narrowness; slow speed; angular and arcade connections; closed 'o' and 'a'; upright or left slant; covering strokes
Inquisitive	High diacritics; pointed tops to M/Z letters; tall, pointed U/Z loops
Inscrutable	Calligraphic or italic script; arcade connections; covering strokes; slow speed
Insecure	Amended letters; light or varying pressure; left slant; narrow word spacing; small PPI
Insensitive	Angular connections; no loops in U/Z or L/Z; heavy pressure; thick, blunt t crosses; very connected

Insincere	Arcade connections; signature different from rest of script; slow speed; narrowness; covering strokes; pseudo-garlands; amended letters
Intelligent	Quick speed; simplified; clever linking; good layout; clear spacing; pointed tops to M/Z letters; well-developed U/Z
Intense	Very heavy pressure on downstrokes; very connected; long L/Z; angular connections; small size; narrowness; excessively straight baseline
Interfering	Words and lines close together; narrow margins; right slant; rightward tendencies
Intolerant	Angular connections; narrowness; narrow or no left margin; potlids; downstrokes of M/Z extending below baseline; PPI in shape of figure 4
Introvert	Left slant; small size; narrowness; tightly knotted 'o' and 'a'
Intuitive	Disconnected; tall U/Z; long L/Z; generally threaded writing; needle-pointed tops of 'm' and 'n'; light pressure; generally loopy; some arcade connections
Inventive	Disconnected; simplified; original letter forms; clear spacing; quick speed
Irresponsible	Concave or weak t crosses; irregular baseline; varying size of M/Z letters
Irritable	Angular connections; heavy or varied pressure; pointed loops in U/Z and L/Z; PPI like figure 4; ticks on starting strokes; sharp or thick t crosses
Jealous	Extreme left or right slant; 'a' and 'o' larger than other M/Z letters; hooks on t crosses or endstrokes; heavy or varying pressure
Jolly	Large size; garland connections; rising lines and endstrokes; wavy t crosses; curved i dots; right slant

j

179

Judgement (good)	Upright; balanced zones; connected; 'g' and 'y' written like 9 and 7; simplified; distinct pressure
Just	*See* Fair-minded

k

Killjoy	Small size; narrowness; down-pointing t crosses; covering strokes; falling lines; PPI like figure 4
Kind	Right slant; garland connections; narrow margins; rounded letter forms; fullness; rightward tendencies; extended endstrokes; fairly disconnected
Know-all	Tall capitals and PPI; tall U/Z; underlined signature; open 'a' and 'o'; narrow word spacing; connected
Knowledgeable	*See* Learned

l

Law-abiding	Good layout; straight left margin; medium size; regular; upright or right slant
Lazy	Upright; slow speed; rounded M/Z; starting strokes; short L/Z; light pressure; irregular spacing; illegible; crowding of words towards end of page
Leader	Large size; heavy pressure; right slant; well sustained horizontal tension; good layout
Learned	Greek form of 'e', 'd' and 'g'; simplified; small size; clear spacing; dominant U/Z; good layout
Lecherous	Smeary strokes with heavy pressure; very long, inflated L/Z; mingling; connected
Lethargic	*See* Listless
Level-headed	Upright; regular; straight baseline; balanced zones; firm or distinct pressure
Listless	Short L/Z; light or varying pressure; weak t crosses; falling lines
Literary	Greek form of letters 'e', 'd' and 'g'; block capitals; upright; fairly disconnected

180

Lively	*See* Vivacious
Logical	Connected; regular; small size; right slant; simplified
Lovable	Garland connections; right slant; rounded U/Z and L/Z loops; broadness; open 'o' and 'a'; extended endstrokes
Loyal	Upright or slight right slant; regular; legible; signature matching rest of script; straight baseline; arcade connections
Luxury-loving	Pasty; fullness; large size; wide margins; long, full L/Z loops; wide spacing; broadness
Lying	*See* Dishonest
Malicious	*See* Spiteful
Manipulative	Thread connections; letters decreasing in size at end of words; flattened arcades; fairly disconnected
Martyr-type	Right-tending L/Z loops; loops in U/Z; small size; very small 'i' in the middle of word
Masochistic	Pasty; well developed L/Z; return stroke of L/Z loop of 'g' and 'y' rising through M/Z oval into U/Z
Materialistic	Dominant L/Z, with inflated loops; pasty; some letters written as figures
Maternal	Roofing strokes on t crosses; rounded letter forms; garland connections; long endstrokes
Mathematical ability	'g' and 'y' written like 9 and 7; leanness; simplified; small size
Mature	High F/S; quick speed; angular connections; clear spacing generally; simplified; originality of letter forms
Mean	Narrowness; small size; no endstrokes; hooks; narrow spacing; narrow margins or no margins; words close together

m

Meditative	Clear, wide word and line spacing; rhythmic; dominant U/Z; leftward tendencies in U/Z; small M/Z
Meek	*See* Submissive
Megalomaniac	Excessively large size; very large capitals, PPI and signature
Melancholic	Falling baseline; irregular; very heavy pressure; small size; signature cancelled through M/Z letters
Memory (aural)	Connected; accurate diacritics; small size; clear word and line spacing
Memory (visual)	As above, with pasty pressure
Mercenary	Very inflated L/Z loops; capital 'L' like £, or 'S' like dollar sign; pasty
Methodical	*See* Systematic
Meticulous	*See* Painstaking
Miserly	*See* Mean
Modest	Small size; small signature and PPI; simplified; small capitals
Moody	*See* Temperamental
Musical	U/Z loops inflated; some musical symbols used; right slant; regular; connected; rhythmic; regular spacing between downstrokes
n Nagging	Triangles in L/Z loops; connected; knots, hooks and ticks; narrow spacing
Naive	Open 'a' and 'o'; letters increasing in size at end of words; garland connections; rounded M/Z
Narrow-minded	Narrowness; short endstrokes; narrow spacing; covering strokes; compressed loops; arcade connections

Nature lover	Pasty; loops in U/Z and L/Z; fullness; broadness
Negative	*See* Defeatist
Nervous	Varying pressure; amended letters; trembling strokes; points on U/Z and L/Z loops; narrowness
Nonchalant	Regular; rhythmic; upright; wide spacing; no loops; simplified
Nosy	*See* Inquisitive
Objective	Leanness; upright; small, clear script; quick speed; sharp angles on some M/Z letters; simplified; regular
Obliging	Right slant; rightward tendencies in L/Z; extended endstrokes; garland connections; broadness
Observant	Fairly disconnected; small or medium size; initial capital letter separated from rest of word
Obsessive	Angular connections; hooks and knots; narrowness; very regular; excessively straight baseline
Obstinate	Hooks on endstrokes and t crosses; heavy pressure; angles in L/Z; potlids; right slant with leftward tendencies
Obstructive	Disconnected; broadness, with low F/S; enriched capitals; superfluous strokes; starting strokes
Obtrusive	Narrow margins; mingling; narrow word spacing; no paragraphs; every available space filled with words
Odd	*See* Eccentric
Offhand	Short or clipped endstrokes; irregular left margin; upright or left slant; wide word spacing; 'o' and 'a' closed
Open	*See* Genuine

o

Open-minded	Upright or right slant; garland connections; broadness; open 'a' and 'o'; long endstrokes; points on some M/Z letters
Opinionated	Tall capitals; tall PPI; inflated U/Z; heavy downstrokes; upright; enriched capitals
Opportunist	Quick speed; clever linking; connected; right slant; simplified; some thread connections
Optimist	Rising lines; rising t crosses; high i dots; right slant; broadness; rising endstrokes
Organizer	Clear word and line spacing; accurate diacritics; legible; good layout; straight baseline; regular
Original	Original and artistic letter forms; disconnected; high F/S; pasty; fullness
Ostentatious	Over-enriched script; large PPI; narrow word spacing; heavily underlined or ornate signature; pasty or heavy pressure
Outspoken	*See* Forthright
Overpowering	*See* Domineering
Overworked	Falling lines; irregular baseline; drooping garlands; signature to left of page; small L/Z; varying pressure; thread connections in middle of words

p

Painstaking	Small or medium size; even pressure; accurate diacritics; balanced margins; 'o' and 'a' closed; knotted loops; slow speed; regular; starting strokes; amended letters
Passionate	Marked right or left slant; large size; some angles; pasty or heavy pressure; inflated U/Z and L/Z loops; irregular
Paternal	Roofing strokes; completed loops in U/Z and L/Z; long endstrokes
Patient	Regular; rhythmic; accurate diacritics; rounded, completed loops in U/Z and L/Z; garland connections; slow speed

Patronizing	Tall capitals and PPI; large size; high, long t crosses to right of stem; descending humps on capital 'M'
Pedantic	Small size; accurate diacritics; some angular connections; connected; regular; amended letters; slow speed
Penetrating mind	Quick speed; sharp pressure; points on U/Z loops; points on M/Z letters; sharp t crosses; leanness
Perceptive	Disconnected; sharp and/or light pressure; points on some M/Z letters and U/Z loops; wide spacing
Perfectionist	Angular and arcade connections; accurate diacritics; regular; very small size, or small size with dominant M/Z; good layout; clear spacing; simplified
Persistent	Straight baseline; firm downstrokes; hooks on endstrokes and t crosses; angular connections; knots on t crosses and L/Z loops; firm pressure; regular
Persuasive	Letters decreasing in size at end of words; thread connections; flattened arcades
Perverse	*See* Wilful
Pessimistic	Falling baseline; weak pressure; weak diacritics; arcade connections
Philanderer	Pasty pressure; large capitals; open 'a' and 'o'; small L/Z; quick speed; large PPI; garland and some thread connections; letters decreasing in size at end of words
Philanthropist	Rightward-tending L/Z loops; right slant; broadness; extended endstrokes; altruistic loops
Phlegmatic	Upright; slow speed; closed 'o' and 'a'; regular; rhythmic; straight baseline; wide word spacing
Placid	Rhythmic; regular; light or medium pressure; rounded letter forms; garland connections

Plausible	Pseudo-garlands; right slant; thread connections; letters decreasing in size at end of words; flattened arcades
Poetic tastes	Rising, curled endstrokes, especially on 'e', 'w' and 'd'; disconnected; pasty or light pressure; Greek form of 'e', 'd' and 'g'
Poised	Upright; tall, simplified capitals; straight baseline; clear spacing; regular; arcade connections
Polite	*See* Courteous
Pompous	Tall capitals and PPI; over-enriched script and signature; no humour signs; large size
Possessive	Medium or heavy pressure; thick endstrokes; t crosses with upturned hooks; left slant; ticks, hooks or knots; enlarged 'o' and/or 'a' in middle of words
Practical	Straight baseline; short U/Z and long L/Z; short endstrokes; arcade connections; narrow margins; narrow word spacing; medium size; square letter forms
Precise	*See* Accurate
Prejudiced	Endstrokes descending vertically below baseline; potlids; extreme right or left slant
Pressured	*See* Overworked
Pretentious	Large, over-enriched capitals and signature; large size; dominant U/Z; arcade connections
Procrastinating	Many starting strokes; diacritics to left of stem; slow speed
Progressive	Right slant; quick speed; rising baseline; rightward tendencies; high diacritics; clever linking; broadness
Promiscuous	Pasty; straight, long L/Z ending in light pressure; marked variety in L/Z formations; mingling

Protective	Roofing strokes; completed loops in U/Z and L/Z; left or right slant; extended endstrokes
Provident	Small size; narrow margins; narrowness; arcade connections; leanness in L/Z loops
Prudent	Upright or left slant; rather slow speed; carefully placed diacritics; narrowing left margin; letters decreasing in size at end of words; closed 'a' and 'o'
Psychic ability	Light pressure; disconnected, or connected with light pressure on connecting strokes; leftward tendencies in L/Z; 'g' like figure 8; thread connections; tall U/Z
Punctual	Accurate, low diacritics; good layout; even left margin; 'g' like figure 8; regular; wide spacing
Quarrelsome	Long, straight starting strokes from below baseline; angular connections; sharp t crosses, often down-pointing; points on U/Z and L/Z loops; angles and triangles on L/Z loops
Quick-tempered	*See* Irritable
Quick-witted	Quick speed; no starting strokes; disconnected; sharp t crosses; simplified; clever linking
Rash	Quick speed; extreme right slant; narrow right margin; widening left margin; t crosses long and to right of stem; broadness with light pressure
Rational	*See* Logical
Realistic	*See* Practical
Rebel	Reversed letters; omitted i dots; counter-strokes; potlids; original letter forms
Relaxed	Very garlanded connections; rhythmic; regular; rounded loops in U/Z and L/Z; distinct pressure
Reliable	Upright; straight baseline; regularity of slant, size and pressure; clear spacing; balanced

q

r

	zones; firm t crosses; medium or high F/S; legible script and signature; well developed L/Z
Religious	Tall, lean U/Z; light pressure; endstrokes rising into U/Z; cruciform 't's; small letter 'k' larger than other M/Z letters
Repressed	Slow speed; narrowness; angular and arcade connections; very narrow loops; closed 'o' and 'a'; covering strokes
Resentful	Long, straight starting strokes from below baseline; small size; narrowness; angular connections; pointed loops
Reserved	Small size; wide word spacing; narrowness; closed 'o' and 'a'; arcade connections; upright or left slant; small capitals and PPI
Resilient	Broadness; small size; simplified; even pressure; same letter written in different ways
Resourceful	Disconnected; clear spacing; original letter forms; broadness; small size; simplified; few or no starting strokes
Respectful	Balanced margins; clear spacing; good layout; legible; ascending humps on capital 'M'; medium size; fairly low diacritics
Responsible	Upright; regular; straight baseline; balanced zones; clear spacing; even pressure; no leftward tendencies in L/Z; arcade connections; simplified
Responsive	Broadness; pasty; garland and thread connections; open 'a' and 'o'; simplified; medium size; fairly connected; right slant
Restless	Uneven pressure, size and slant; amended letters; long L/Z loops or single strokes; rather disconnected; uneven spacing; mingling
Retiring	Small M/Z; small PPI; wide right margin; closed 'o' and 'a'; mingling in M/Z letters; wide word spacing

Rigid	*See* Inflexible
Romantic	Right or left slant; garland connections; tall U/Z; loops in U/Z and L/Z; pasty
Rude	Irregular left margin; poor layout; illegible; erratic word spacing; omitted i dots; mingling
Ruthless	Narrowness; angular connections; compressed loops or straight, single downstrokes in L/Z; heavy pressure; large capitals and PPI; signature underlined
Sad	Falling baseline; no endstrokes; low, weak t crosses; small M/Z
Sadistic	Heavy or pasty pressure; blunt t crosses; angular connections; return stroke of L/Z loop of 'g' and 'y' rising through M/Z oval into U/Z
Sarcastic	Very sharp t crosses, often down-pointing; sharpness generally; light pressure; angular connections
Scatter-brained	*See* Feather-brained
Sceptical	Upright; arcade connections; narrowness; connected
Scheming	*See* Devious
Secretive	Closed and knotted 'o', 'a' and 'd'; illegible signature; arcade connections; covering strokes; narrowness
Self-assured	*See* Self-confident
Self-centred	Narrowness; mingling; large PPI; upright or left slant; large M/Z; uneven spacing; varying pressure; uneven left margin
Self-confident	Tall, simplified capitals; underlined signature; quick speed; large size, especially M/Z; firm pressure; upright; large PPI
Self-conscious	Left slant; small size; slow speed; narrowness; amended PPI

s

Self-contained	Upright; wide word and line spacing; connected; closed 'o' and 'a'; arcade connections
Self-controlled	*See* Self-disciplined
Self-protective	Endstrokes rising and tending leftwards over previous letter, particularly 'd' and 'w'; endstroke of signature extending over whole name, or signature entirely circled
Self-destructive	*See* Suicidal tendencies
Self-disciplined	Upright; regular; straight baseline; firm, even pressure; clear spacing; simplified; convex t crosses
Self-important	*See* Pompous
Self-indulgent	Concave t crosses; large size, or dominant M/Z; broadness; pasty; narrow word spacing
Selfish	Dominant M/Z; hooked endstrokes; large, enriched PPI; large capitals; flourished, underlined signature; pasty; upright or left slant; uneven spacing; varying pressure
Self-possessed	*See* Poised
Self-satisfied	*See* Smug
Self-sufficient	*See* Independent
Sensible	Upright; connected; straight baseline; firm pressure; regular; balanced zones
Sensitive	Looped, sharp t crosses; endstrokes rising and tending leftwards; light or varying pressure; irregular baseline and script; left or mixed slant
Sensual	Heavy or very pasty pressure; inflated or ink-filled loops; some angles in a dominant L/Z; enriched capitals; concave t crosses
Sensuous	Pasty; right slant; well developed U/Z and L/Z loops

Sentimental	Irregular; pasty; large M/Z with fullness; marked right or left slant; inflated loops
Serene	Rhythmic; regular; light pressure; garland connections; rounded letter forms
Servile	Low t crosses; small capitals; thread connections; low F/S; flattened arcades
Severe	Angular connections; sharpness; narrowness; leanness in all three zones; firm pressure
Shallow	Dominant M/Z; concave t crosses; signature with wavy underlining
Shifty	Irregular baseline; closed and knotted 'o' and 'a'; covering strokes; thread and wavy line connections; flattened arcades
Shrewd	Angular connections; sharpness; closed 'o' and 'a'; short endstrokes; upright; some thread connections
Shy	Wide right margin; small size; closed 'o' and 'a'; left slant; narrowness; small capitals and signature
Simple	*See* Naive
Sincere	Quick speed; straight baseline; open 'o' and 'a'; right slant; legible script; signature same as rest of script
Single-minded	Right slant; no starting strokes; firm downstrokes; connected; good horizontal tension
Sly	Thread connections; varying size of M/Z letters; irregular baseline; pseudo-garlands; illegible signature; knotted 'o' and 'a'; covering strokes; counter-strokes
Smug	Vanity loops; large capitals and PPI; large involved signature; dominant M/Z
Snobbish	Tall capitals; large PPI; upright; very wide left margin; angular connections; t crosses flying upwards

Sociable	Right slant; broadness; connected; open 'a' and 'o'; garland connections; legible script
Solitary	Wide word and line spacing; disconnected; small size; signature placed at some distance from rest of script
Sophisticated	Arcade connections; upright; slow speed; straight baseline; regular; tall, simplified capitals
Spendthrift	Widening left margin; broadness; large capitals; wide word spacing; pasty
Spiritual	*See* Religious
Spiteful	Sharp t crosses, often down-pointing; angular connections; pointed loops in U/Z and L/Z; sharpness; narrowness
Spoilt	Large M/Z; wide word and line spacing; low or medium F/S; concave t crosses; roundness generally
Spontaneous	*See* Genuine
Straightforward	*See* Direct
Strong-minded	Heavy pressure; long, well-developed L/Z; regular; strong t crosses; clear spacing; straight baseline; angular connections
Stubborn	*See* Obstinate
Submissive	Small size; light pressure; small capitals; capital 'I' written as small letter; narrowness; low t crosses; monotonous roundness of script
Suicidal tendencies	Falling baseline; wide word and line spacing; signature on left of page and address on far left of envelope; varying pressure; endstroke of signature to left; signature cancelled through M/Z letters
Superficial	*See* Shallow
Suspicious	Upright or left slant; full stop after signature; narrowness; covering strokes

Sympathetic	Fairly disconnected; right slant; garland connections; altruistic loops; broadness; narrow word spacing
Systematic	Accurate diacritics; small size; straight baseline; regular; balanced margins; good layout; simplified
Taciturn	Closed and knotted 'o', 'a' and 'd'; 't' written **t** with gap between upstroke and downstroke; clipped endstrokes; narrow margins; narrowness; arcade connections
Tactful	Closed 'o' and 'a'; letters at end of words decreasing in size; thread connections
Tactless	Open 'o' and 'a'; letters at end of words increasing in size; short or clipped endstrokes
Talkative	Open 'o', 'a' and 'd'; very connected; broadness; rising baseline; garland and thread connections; narrow margins and spacing
Teaching ability	Rounded, completed loops in U/Z and L/Z; the second of double letters taller than the first; broadness
Technical ability	Leanness; small size; square letter forms; accurate diacritics; entire script in block capitals, with high or medium F/S
Temperamental	Mixed slant; irregular; varying pressure; irregular baseline; mixture of rising and falling lines
Tenacious	Hooks on t crosses and endstrokes; angular connections; sharpness; firm downstrokes; regular; heavy pressure
Tense	Extreme narrowness; amended letters; angular connections; points on U/Z and L/Z loops; varying pressure
Thorough	Heavy pressure; knots and hooks; loops on U/Z; accurate diacritics; small size; some starting strokes
Thoughtless	*See* Inconsiderate

Thrifty	*See* Economical
Tidy	Good layout; straight margins; regular; accurate diacritics; small size; regular word spacing
Timid	Light pressure; small size; narrow left margin; wide right margin; small PPI; narrowness; trembling strokes; weak t crosses
Tolerant	Garland connections; broadness; rounded loops in U/Z and L/Z; upright; short t crosses; regular; rhythmic
Touchy	*See* Sensitive
Traveller	Broadness; pasty or distinct pressure; upright or right slant; high i dots
Trendy	Circle i dots; pasty; wide U/Z loops; artistically ornamented script; use of unusual ink colours
Trustworthy	Straight baseline; very legible; regular; even word and line spacing; balanced zones; straight left margin
Truthful	*See* Honest
Two-faced	*See* Hypocritical
u Unassuming	Small size; small PPI and signature; simplified
Unbiased	*See* Unprejudiced
Uncharitable	*See* Unkind
Uncommunicative	*See* Taciturn
Uncompromising	Angular connections; firm downstrokes; convex t crosses; knotted loops; potlids; hooks or ticks on starting and endstrokes
Unconventional	Mixed slant; disconnected; circle i dots; large M/Z; use of unusual ink colours; original letter forms

Undemonstrative	Narrowness; small size; absence of loops; upright
Undisciplined	Mixed slant; irregular baseline; mingling; concave t crosses; varying size of M/Z letters; poor spacing and layout
Unfaithful	Varying size, slant and pressure; irregular baseline; concave t crosses; irregular; mingling; garland and thread connections
Unfeeling	Sharp pressure; angular connections; narrowness; leanness; upright; compressed loops
Unkind	Poor word spacing; angular connections; sharp, down-pointing t crosses; uneven left margin; letters increasing in size at end of words
Unpredictable	Mixed slant; irregular baseline; mingling; irregular; thread connections
Unprejudiced	Upright; balanced zones; broadness; straight baseline; clear spacing; simplified
Unprincipled	*See* Immoral
Unreliable	Irregular baseline; small L/Z; mixed slant; irregular; covering strokes; varying pressure; mingling
Unscrupulous	Some M/Z letters open at baseline; angular connections; over-inflated L/Z; large PPI; large size; signature different from rest of script; small U/Z
Unselfish	Right slant; simplified; small size; regular; garland connections; clear spacing
Unsettled	*See* Restless
Untidy	Irregular; mingling; poor layout; omitted diacritics; mixed slant; uneven word spacing
Unyielding	*See* Uncompromising
Urbane	Pseudo-garlands; right slant; thread connections; letters decreasing in size at end

		of words; pasty; large M/Z
v	Vacillating	Mixed slant; varying pressure; irregular; t crosses concave or to left of stem; gap between last letter of word and preceding letters; thread connections
	Vain	*See* Conceited
	Versatile	Original letter forms; fairly disconnected; thread connections; mixed slant with high F/S; same letter written in different ways
	Vindictive	Loops pointed in U/Z and L/Z; triangles in L/Z loops; angular connections; heavy pressure; very sharp t crosses
	Violent tendencies	Heavy pressure; clubbed t crosses; very thick downstrokes; thick, heavy endstrokes turning downwards; very connected; angles and triangles in L/Z
	Vitality	Quick speed; rising lines; firm pressure; broadness; right slant; long, well-developed L/Z; diacritics to right of stem; simplified
	Vivacious	Quick speed; broadness; pasty; rising lines; right slant; high or rising t crosses; high i dots; tall capitals
	Volatile	Mixed slant; irregular baseline; rising endstrokes; variations in all three zones; variety of connections; varying pressure
	Voyeur	Smeary strokes; dominant L/Z, very long or with extended leftward tendencies; covering strokes; counter-strokes; involved PPI
	Vulgar	Heavy pressure; large, ornate capitals and signature; over-enriched script; irregular spacing; illegible; poor layout
	Vulnerable	Light pressure; garland connections; rounded letter forms; no angles
w	Warm-hearted	Right slant; pasty pressure; long L/Z; broadness; garland connections

Wary	*See* Cautious
Waspish	*See* Irritable
Wasteful	*See* Extravagant
Wavering	*See* Vacillating
Weak-willed	Irregular; mixed slant; weak pressure; short, low or concave t crosses; mingling
Weary	Light or varying pressure; weak diacritics; drooping garlands; falling words at end of lines; small L/Z
Whimsical	*See* Capricious
Wilful	Hooks on endstrokes and t crosses; heavy pressure; angular connections; potlids; omitted i dots; reversed letters
Willpower	Regular; firm pressure; strong, high t crosses; clear spacing; straight or rising baseline; hooks on endstrokes
Wise	Upright; tall U/Z; points on M/Z letters; simplified; 'g' and 'y' like figures 9 and 7; fairly disconnected
Withdrawn	*See* Solitary
Witty	Fairly connected; open 'a' and 'o'; sharp and/or wavy t crosses; curved i dots
Worrying type	Falling baseline; points on loops; amended letters and words; words very close together; narrowness
Yes-man	Flattened arcades; letters decreasing in size at end of words; thread connections; pseudo-garlands; low F/S; low t crosses
Yielding	Small size; light pressure; small capitals and PPI; low t crosses; rounded letter forms; garland connections
Zany	Slow speed; amended letters; enriched capitals; mingling; open 'a' and 'o'; low F/S; garland connections; wavy t crosses.

y

z

Zealous	Quick speed; fairly heavy pressure; t crosses high and to right of stem; angular connections; right slant; rising baseline; connected
Zestful	Quick speed; rising lines; large size; broadness; right slant; long, high t crosses to right of stem; rising endstrokes

Glossary

Altruistic loops	*See* Loops	
Amended letters	Letters retouched after initial formation, indicating anxiety states or neurotic tendencies	*Retouched*
Angles	*See* Loops	
Angular	*See* Forms of connection *and* Loops	
Arcade	*See* Forms of connection	
Artificial fullness	*See* Style	
Arhythmic	*See* Rhythm	
Baseline	Invisible horizontal line on which writing stands, indicating degree of reliability and emotional balance	
	Rising	*Rising lines*
	Straight	*Straight*
	Falling	*Falling lines*
	Irregular	*Irregular*
Block capitals		A B C D E F
Broadness	*See* Horizontal width	
Cancelling out	*See* Signature	
Claws	*See* Strokes	

Clever linking   *See* Connectedness

Concave t cross   *See* Diacritics

Connectedness   Degree of connection
                      between letters; an
                      indication of the type
                      of thinking process

    Connected (five or   *Connected*
    more letters
    connected in one
    word): logical
    thinking

    Connected words: *Where are you*
    fluency of thought

    Clever linking: *This is true*
    ability to combine
    ideas

    Disconnected (four   *Disconnected*
    or fewer letters
    connected in one
    word): reliance on
    intuition

Consequential   *See* A–Z, p. 60
'I'

Convex t cross   *See* Diacritics

Copybook   Style of writing as
                      taught at school.
                      Adherence to, or
                      departure from,
                      copybook forms shows
                      degree of conformity
                      or originality

Counter-strokes   Consistent distortion
                      of copybook forms,
                      indicating dishonesty,

Counter-strokes *contd.*	hypocrisy or concealment	
	M/Z ovals open on baseline	*d o a bg*
	Distorted letter forms	*n nc o* (n) (m) (o)
	Double-walling	*a o d*
Covering strokes	Upstrokes covered by downstrokes and vice versa, showing repressed emotions	*flowing*
Diacritics	Collective term for i dots and t crosses	
	Accurate	*quite right*
	Inaccurate	*inaccurate*
	Concave (t cross)	*tempted*
	Convex (t cross)	*not tempted*
	Clubbed (t cross)	*brutality*
	Dash (i dot)	*impatience*

Diligence loops	*See* Loops
Disconnectedness	*See* Connectedness
Distinct pressure	*See* Pressure
Double-walling	*See* Counter-strokes
Endstrokes	*See* Strokes

Enriched	*See* Simplification
Flattened arcades	*See* Forms of connection
Forms of connection	Connecting strokes between letters, showing social attitudes and/or mental agility

Angular: inflexible, decisive

angular

Arcade: reserved, practical

underneath

Flattened arcades: a bluffer

flattering

Garland: friendly, receptive

friendliness

Deep: tendency to dramatize

waiting

Drooping: under pressure, overworked

under lines

Pseudo: effusive, insincere

ïïindoïïs

Shallow: frivolous

shallow

Thread: quick mind, creative

thread writing

Glossary

Forms of connection *contd.*	Wavy line: diplomatic, conciliatory	*wavy line*
F/S (Form standard)	Standard of writing as judged by speed, naturalness, originality, layout etc. Considered together, these show degree of integration of spiritual, physical and instinctual drives	
	High	*The Prince of Wales.*
	Medium	*very happy the weather*
	Low	*However, my to come.*
Fullness	*See* Style	
Garland connections	*See* Forms of connection	
Greek form		*d ε g*
Hooks	*See* Strokes	
Horizontal tension	Pull of writing towards the right, showing ambition, drive and executive ability	
	Strong	*pull to right*
	Slack	*weak tension*

Horizontal width	Broadness or narrowness of letters, indicating extent of expansiveness or restriction of personality	
	Broadness	*broadness*
	Narrowness	*narrowness*
Irregular	*See* Regularity	
i dots	*See* Diacritics	
Knots	*See* Strokes	
Lateral pressure	*See* Pressure	
Layout	Arrangement of writing on page, indicating aesthetic appreciation and general attitude towards society	*This is a good arrangement of writing on the page.*
Leanness	*See* Style	
Leftward tendencies	*See* Tendencies	
Loops	In any zone, an indication of strength of emotional responses	
	Average, wide, compressed	*ℓ ℓ ℓ*
	No loop/single stroke	*ι ι q*
	Angles/angular/ triangular	*ℓ g g*

Loops *contd.*	Altruistic	*q (g) y (y)*
	Diligence	*d b p*
	Vanity	*t d*
L/Z (Lower zone)	*See* Zones	
Mingling	*See* Spacing	
Mixed slant	*See* Slant	
M/Z (Middle zone)	*See* Zones	
Narrowness	*See* Horizontal width	
Neglected	*See* Simplification	
Ovals	Letters, or parts of letters, in M/Z, normally round or oval in shape	*a d e g o q*
Over-enriched	*See* Simplification	
Pasty	*See* Pressure	
Potlids	*See* Strokes	
PPI (Personal Pronoun 'I')	Shows writer's feelings about himself and his role in society (see Part I: A–Z)	
Pressure	Pressure of pen and quality of stroke, indicating degree of physical and emotional energy and moral strength	
	Heavy	*Heavy*

Pressure *contd.*	Medium	*Medium*
	Light	*Light*
	Varying	*Varying*
	Pasty	*Pastiness*
	Smeary	*Smeary*
	Sharp	*Sharp*
	Distinct	*Shading*
	Lateral	*Lateral*
Printed letters	Printed small letters (not block capitals)	*printed*
Pseudo-garlands	*See* Forms of connection	
Regularity	Uniformity of slant, size of M/Z and distance between downstrokes, indicating measure of self-control and emotional discipline	
	Regular	*Regular*
	Irregular	*Irregular*
Reversed letters	Letters drawn in the reverse direction from copybook, showing contrariness,	*t₂ (t₂) ↑ (ℐ)*

Reversed letters *contd.*	rebelliousness – a desire to be different
Rhythm	Natural flow and overall harmony of writing on page, demonstrating placidity or restlessness of temperament
	Rhythmic
	Arhythmic
Rightward tendencies	*See* Tendencies
Roofing strokes	Strokes extended over the whole or part of a word, showing a desire to protect or patronize
Sharp	*See* Pressure
Signature	Projection of writer's self-image; status symbol
	Rising: professional ambition
	Cancelled out through M/Z: acute depression, suicidal tendencies
	Underlined: self-confidence
	Enriched: artistic appreciation or

Signature *contd.*	attention-seeking behaviour	
	Illegible: desire to misrepresent or hide one's true self	
Simplification/ Enrichment	Omission of unnecessary strokes while retaining legibility, or embellishments to enhance appearance. Indicates degree of intelligence, grasp of essentials, taste and artistic appreciation	
	Simplified	
	Neglected	
	Enriched	
	Over-enriched	
Single strokes	*See* Loops	
Size	Expression of writer's view of the world, the importance of his place in it, and his desire for recognition. Average, or medium, size: three millimetres per zone	
	Small (less than 9 mm)	

Size *contd.*	Large (9½ to 11 mm)	*large*
	Very large (more than 11½ mm)	*largest*
Slant	Angle of writing in relation to baseline, indicating social adjustment and emotional expression	
	Right: sociable	*right slant*
	Marked right: impulsive	*marked right*
	Upright: independent	*upright*
	Left: cautious, reserved	*left slant*
	Marked left: withdrawn	*marked left*
	Mixed: unpredictable	*mixed slant*
Smeary	*See* Pressure	
Spacing	Distance between words, representing distance the writer likes to maintain between himself and others	
	Distance between lines, an indication of	

Spacing *contd.*	mental clarity and orderliness	
	Wide	*wide word and line spacing*
	Narrow	*narrow word and line spacing*
	Mingling	*mingling of the lines*
Speed	Writing speed can be equated with speed of reaction and response. It is judged by certain characteristics:	
	Quick Broadness; connectedness; diacritics to right; light pressure; rising baseline; right slant; simplified; widening left margin	
	Slow Narrowness; disconnectedness; diacritics to left; heavy pressure; falling baseline; upright or left slant; enriched; narrowing left margin	
	Quick	*Speedy writing*
	Medium	*medium speed*
	Slow	*Slow writing*
Starting strokes	*See* Strokes	

Strokes	Any movement additional to the basic letter form	
	Starting strokes	*starting stroke*
	Endstrokes	*endstroke*
	Hooks, claws	*hooks, clawing*
	Knots	*Knotting*
	Ticks	*ticks and*
	Potlids	*potlids*
	Trembling, bent, broken strokes	*bent breaking trembling*
Style	Amount of space enclosed within outline of letter, indicating degree of emotional and imaginative response to experience	
	Fullness	*Emotional*
	Leanness	*leanness*
	Artificial fullness	*fantasy*
t crosses	*See* Diacritics	
Tendencies	Movements with or against flow of writing, revealing attitude towards	

Tendencies *contd.*	other people and the future, or towards the ego and the past
	Rightward (future) *Rightward*
	Leftward (past) *Leftward*
Thread	*See* Forms of connection
Ticks	*See* Strokes
Triangles	*See* Loops
Upright	*See* Slant
U/Z (Upper zone)	*See* Zones
Vanity loops	*See* Loops
Wavy line	*See* Forms of connection
Zones	Division of letters into three zones (upper, middle and lower), corresponding to three areas in a person's life. Balance of zones is an indication of inner equilibrium and maturity
	U/Z: mind, spirit and imagination
	M/Z: social self, involvement in day-to-day activity *happy*
	L/Z: unconscious, instinctual drives

Recommended Reading

Amend, Karen and Ruiz, Mary S., *The Complete Book of Handwriting Analysis*, Newcastle Publishing Co., Hollywood, 1980; as *Handwriting Analysis: The Complete Basic Book*, London, 1980.

Friedenhain, Paula, *Write and Reveal: Interpretation of Handwriting*, Humanities Press, New York, 1973; Peter Owen, London, 1973.

Gardner, Ruth, *A Graphology Student's Workbook*, Llewellyn Publications, St Paul, Minnesota, 1975.

Hartford, Huntington, *You Are What You Write: Comprehensive Guide to Handwriting Analysis*, Macmillan Publishing Co., New York, 1973; Peter Owen, London, 1975.

Hill, Barbara, *Graphology*, Robert Hale, London, 1981.

Hughes, Albert E., *What Your Handwriting Reveals*, Neville Spearman, London, 1970; Wilshire Book Co., Hollywood, 1978; Sphere Books, London, 1980.

Marne, Patricia, *Crime and Sex in Handwriting*, Constable, London, 1981.

——, *Graphology*, Hodder & Stoughton, London, 1980.

Meyer, Jerome S., *The Handwriting Analyzer*, Simon & Schuster, New York, 1974.

Olyanova, Nadya, *Handwriting Tells*, The Bobbs-Merrill Co., New York, 1969; Peter Owen, London, 1974.

——, *The Psychology of Handwriting*, Wilshire Book Co., Hollywood, 1977.

Paterson, Jane, *Interpreting Handwriting*, David McKay Co., New York, 1976

Rockwell, Frances, *Graphology for Lovers*, New American Library, New York, 1979; London, 1980.

Roman, Klara G., *Handwriting: A Key to Personality*, Pantheon Books, New York, 1977.

Sara, Dorothy, *Handwriting Analysis*, Pyramid Books, New York, 1956.

Singer, Eric, *A Manual of Graphology*, Duckworth, London, 1974.

——, *Personality in Handwriting*, Duckworth, London, 1974.

The following pages are left blank
for you to note the sections that apply
to your particular handwriting
(Your friends may also be included if you wish)